DO Drops
Volume 9

DO Drops

Volume 9

Daily Bible Devotional

Dr. Bo Wagner

Word of His Mouth Publishers
Mooresboro, NC

All Scripture quotations are taken from the **King James Version** of the Bible.

ISBN: 978-1-941039-30-4
Printed in the United States of America
©2023 Dr. Bo Wagner

Word of His Mouth Publishers
Mooresboro, NC
www.wordofhismouth.com

Cover art by Chip Nuhrah

Devotion 1

After the death of King Asa, we find another decent king ascending to the throne of Judah.

2 Chronicles 17:1 *And Jehoshaphat his son reigned in his stead, and strengthened himself against Israel.* **2** *And he placed forces in all the fenced cities of Judah, and set garrisons in the land of Judah, and in the cities of Ephraim, which Asa his father had taken.* **3** *And the LORD was with Jehoshaphat, because he walked in the first ways of his father David, and sought not unto Baalim;* **4** *But sought to the LORD God of his father, and walked in his commandments, and not after the doings of Israel.*

We once again in this text find another instance of free will and consequences. King Jehoshaphat had a choice; seek after Jehovah or seek after Baalim, walk after the commandments of God or walk in the wickedness of the northern kingdom of Israel. He chose to do right; he chose to seek God. And verse three tells us that God was with him because of that.

This paradigm has never changed, whether Old Testament or New Testament. Simply put, the law of sowing and reaping applies in any dispensation. We can either choose to do right or we can choose to do wrong, and God will either bless us or blister us accordingly.

This is just one more thing that makes it a very good reason to do right, so DO right!

Personal Notes:

_____
_____
_____
_____
_____
_____
_____
_____
_____
_____
_____
_____
_____
_____
_____
_____
_____
_____
_____
_____
_____
_____
_____
_____
_____
_____
_____
_____

Devotion 2

As we continue to examine the reign of Jehoshaphat, we come to a passage that is truly stunning in light of the push in our modern day to remove God from public life.

2 Chronicles 17:5 *Therefore the LORD stablished the kingdom in his hand; and all Judah brought to Jehoshaphat presents; and he had riches and honour in abundance.* **6** *And his heart was lifted up in the ways of the LORD: moreover he took away the high places and groves out of Judah.* **7** *Also in the third year of his reign he sent to his princes, even to Benhail, and to Obadiah, and to Zechariah, and to Nethaneel, and to Michaiah, to teach in the cities of Judah.* **8** *And with them he sent Levites, even Shemaiah, and Nethaniah, and Zebadiah, and Asahel, and Shemiramoth, and Jehonathan, and Adonijah, and Tobijah, and Tobadonijah, Levites; and with them Elishama and Jehoram, priests.* **9** *And they taught in Judah, and had the book of the law of the LORD with them, and went about throughout all the cities of Judah, and taught the people.* **10** *And the fear of the LORD fell upon all the kingdoms of the lands that were round about Judah, so that they made no war against Jehoshaphat.*

The king sent his princes along with religious leaders to teach the citizenry the written word of God. Think "Trump sends Pence and Cruz and McConnell along with Pastor Wagner and Franklin Graham to hold national Bible classes with everyone." Can you imagine the howls and screams of protest from the left? And yet the result of what Jehoshaphat did was *"the fear of the LORD fell upon all the kingdoms of the lands that were round about Judah, so that they made no war against Jehoshaphat."*

Most people do not realize this today, but there are literally Bible verses engraved in stone all across Washington DC. They are silent testimonies to a saner time when America understood that the favor of God on our land could not be lived without.

Much of our land despises the idea of public displays of Christianity nowadays. But whether or not Washington is okay with it, DO publicly display it yourself; if our leaders will not lead, we must lead our leaders!

Personal Notes:

_____

_____

_____

_____

_____

_____

_____

_____

_____

_____

_____

_____

_____

_____

_____

_____

Devotion 3

The closing verses of 2 Chronicles 17 show us the wealth and success of King Jehoshaphat. But by now you should know that the kings of Judah tended not to handle success too very well...

2 Chronicles 18:1 *Now Jehoshaphat had riches and honour in abundance, and joined affinity with Ahab.*

Part one of that verse: yayyyyyy!

Part two of that verse: D'oh!

Jehoshaphat grew strong and his kingdom was prosperous specifically because of righteousness. What in the world, then, made him feel like it was a good idea to become BFFs with very literally the most wicked man in Israeli history, Ahab, who just so happened to be married to the most wicked woman in all of history, Jezebel?

To put this in modern terms, having your right hand in the nail-scarred hand of Christ while having your left hand in the sin-soaked hand of Satan makes no sense whatsoever. Trying to live for God while having wicked, anti-God friends makes no sense whatsoever.

DO choose a side, and DO choose the right one!

Personal Notes:

Devotion 4

After informing us of King Jehoshaphat's foolish alliance with Ahab, the next few verses begin to unfold the disaster that would come from it.

2 Chronicles 18:2 *And after certain years he went down to Ahab to Samaria. And Ahab killed sheep and oxen for him in abundance, and for the people that he had with him, and persuaded him to go up with him to Ramothgilead. 3 And Ahab king of Israel said unto Jehoshaphat king of Judah, Wilt thou go with me to Ramothgilead? And he answered him, I am as thou art, and my people as thy people; and we will be with thee in the war. 4 And Jehoshaphat said unto the king of Israel, Enquire, I pray thee, at the word of the LORD to day.*

Pop quiz time!

Question: When do the words "ask God" (enquire at the word of the Lord) make no sense whatsoever?

Answer: When they are preceded by "I will do whatever you say, Ahab, my best bud!" and when that wicked "best bud," who does not believe in God anyway, is the one that you are asking to "ask God!"

Prayer should come before you make a decision, not after. And prayers should be your own, not someone else's, and certainly not someone who does not even know the God they are praying to!

DO pray your own prayers, and DO especially pray your prayers and hear from God before you make your decisions!

Personal Notes:

_____
_____
_____
_____
_____
_____
_____
_____
_____
_____
_____
_____
_____
_____
_____
_____
_____
_____
_____
_____
_____
_____
_____
_____
_____
_____
_____
_____

Devotion 5

When Jehoshaphat asked Ahab to enquire of the LORD, a "logistical problem" ensued. You see, Ahab did not actually have any prophets of the Lord; all of them had been gotten rid of so that Jezebel could fully install Baal worship in the land. Nonetheless, Ahab did have some "prophets for profit" on the payroll, and they were quickly called in and consulted. Their consent was unanimous, utterly unanimous.

2 Chronicles 18:5 *Therefore the king of Israel gathered together of prophets four hundred men, and said unto them, Shall we go to Ramothgilead to battle, or shall I forbear? And they said, Go up; for God will deliver it into the king's hand.*

Here was the clearly stated prophecy: Ahab and Israel would win the battle they were going into; God would make sure of it.

Let's drop down into the text and see how that worked out.

2 Chronicles 18:33 *And a certain man drew a bow at a venture, and smote the king of Israel between the joints of the harness: therefore he said to his chariot man, Turn thine hand, that thou mayest carry me out of the host; for I am wounded.* **34** *And the battle increased that day: howbeit the king of Israel stayed himself up in his chariot against the Syrians until the even: and about the time of the sun going down he died.*

Summary: Israel lost, and Ahab died. The very clear "prophecy" did not come true, at all. And yet we never read of them being removed, and the next kings in the line of Israel continued to consult them. It seems that in their age, as in ours, "prophets" are much like "climate experts" and "science experts" and "political experts;" they can be wrong over and over again and still be regarded as prophets/experts. We saw this a lot in the last election, where "prophets" assured the world that Donald Trump would be re-inaugurated as president in January 2021. And yet they are still being called prophets.

In old-timey talk, DO "call a spade a spade;" DO call false prophets false prophets!

Personal Notes:

_____
_____
_____
_____
_____
_____
_____
_____
_____
_____
_____
_____
_____
_____
_____
_____
_____
_____

Devotion 6

We often hear lamentations in our day that "Christianity is so needlessly divided and fractured, and we must lay aside doctrine and simply unify around love." Well, as we continue the account of Ahab and Jehoshaphat preparing to join in the battle against the Syrians, we will find nearly 3,000 years ago that same philosophy playing out.

2 Chronicles 18:6 *But Jehoshaphat said, Is there not here a prophet of the LORD besides, that we might enquire of him?* **7** *And the king of Israel said unto Jehoshaphat, There is yet one man, by whom we may enquire of the LORD: but I hate him; for he never prophesied good unto me, but always evil: the same is Micaiah the son of Imla. And Jehoshaphat said, Let not the king say so.* **8** *And the king of Israel called for one of his officers, and said, Fetch quickly Micaiah the son of Imla.* **9** *And the king of Israel and Jehoshaphat king of Judah sat either of them on his throne, clothed in their robes, and they sat in a void place at the entering in of the gate of Samaria; and all the prophets prophesied before them.* **10** *And Zedekiah the son of Chenaanah had made him horns of iron, and said, Thus saith the LORD, With these thou shalt push Syria until they be consumed.* **11** *And all the prophets prophesied so, saying, Go up to Ramothgilead, and prosper: for the LORD shall deliver it into the hand of the king.* **12** *And the messenger that went to call Micaiah spake to him, saying, Behold, the words of the prophets declare good to the king with one assent; let thy word* *therefore, I pray thee, be like one of theirs, and speak thou good.*

Zedekiah and all of his "other preacher buddies" had a unified message. Doctrine had indeed been laid aside; if it had not been, they would have been preaching the exact opposite of what they were preaching! But when a messenger was sent to talk to Micaiah, the "other preacher" in town, he begged him to please only preach what everyone else was preaching...

But everyone else was preaching wrong!

DO understand that our unity must always be based on true biblical doctrine; if it is not, we are unified in the exact same way as everyone who was left on the Titanic after all of the lifeboats were gone!

Personal Notes:

_____

_____

_____

_____

_____

_____

_____

_____

_____

_____

_____

_____

_____

_____

_____

Devotion 7

Micaiah did not play along with the "errbody jest preach the same thang" philosophy. He told Ahab that he was going to die in the coming battle. He also explained why all of the other prophets were unanimous in saying the exact opposite thing:

2 Chronicles 18:18 *Again he said, Therefore hear the word of the LORD; I saw the LORD sitting upon his throne, and all the host of heaven standing on his right hand and on his left.* **19** *And the LORD said, Who shall entice Ahab king of Israel, that he may go up and fall at Ramothgilead? And one spake saying after this manner, and another saying after that manner.* **20** *Then there came out a spirit, and stood before the LORD, and said, I will entice him. And the LORD said unto him, Wherewith?* **21** *And he said, I will go out, and be a lying spirit in the mouth of all his prophets. And the LORD said, Thou shalt entice him, and thou shalt also prevail: go out, and do even so.*

When it comes to "prophets," or preachers, or anyone else who claims to be speaking for God, there are three types you will find. Those who simply speak their own words, those who speak the words of God, and those who speak the words of devils under the actual influence of devils! Those types of people and situations actually do exist and are far more common than most people would be comfortable admitting. This is why it is so essential to know your Bible; nothing that comes from God will ever contradict it!

DO know your Bible and evaluate every message and every messenger from it!

Personal Notes:

_____

_____

_____

_____

_____

_____

_____

_____

_____

_____

_____

_____

_____

_____

_____

_____

_____

_____

_____

_____

_____

_____

_____

_____

_____

_____

_____

_____

_____

_____

_____

Devotion 8

As Micaiah prophesied, Ahab was killed in battle. Jehoshaphat returned home to Judah, doubtless intending to put the entire matter behind him. But though he may have been done with the matter, God certainly was not.

2 Chronicles 19:1 *And Jehoshaphat the king of Judah returned to his house in peace to Jerusalem.* **2** *And Jehu the son of Hanani the seer went out to meet him, and said to king Jehoshaphat, Shouldest thou help the ungodly, and love them that hate the LORD? therefore is wrath upon thee from before the LORD.*

This passage presents an uncomfortable truth to us, but a truth nonetheless: as Christians, we are not allowed to "love" everyone! Jehu said, "Should you love them that hate the LORD?" The answer he was clearly expecting was "No!" In fact, the WRATH of God was up on Jehoshaphat because he did, not the FAVOR of God.

But that brings up some questions, doesn't it? We know that "God so loved the world," and we know that Jesus was regarded as "the friend of sinners." So how do we balance all of that?

It is pretty simple, really. We can love the world the way God loved the world in the sense that He gave Himself for them so that they could be saved. And we can be a friend to sinners who are open to the gospel. But we cannot ever love those that actually HATE God the way that Jehoshaphat loved Ahab. We cannot join hearts and hands and purposes and plans with them. With people who hate God, we must obey the command of God to come out from among them and be separate (2 Corinthians 6:17-18). So DO remember to love God enough not to love those that hate God!

Personal Notes:

_____

_____

_____

_____

_____

_____

_____

_____

_____

_____

_____

_____

_____

_____

_____

_____

_____

_____

_____

_____

_____

_____

_____

_____

Devotion 9

King Jehoshaphat made a mistake by joining affinity with Ahab. And yet, other than that, he was generally a truly good king.

2 Chronicles 19:3 *Nevertheless there are good things found in thee, in that thou hast taken away the groves out of the land, and hast prepared thine heart to seek God.* **4** *And Jehoshaphat dwelt at Jerusalem: and he went out again through the people from Beersheba to mount Ephraim, and brought them back unto the LORD God of their fathers.* **5** *And he set judges in the land throughout all the fenced cities of Judah, city by city,* **6** *And said to the judges, Take heed what ye do: for ye judge not for man, but for the LORD, who is with you in the judgment.* **7** *Wherefore now let the fear of the LORD be upon you; take heed and do it: for there is no iniquity with the LORD our God, nor respect of persons, nor taking of gifts.*

In verse four, we find Jehoshaphat personally going throughout the countryside to speak to his people and encourage them to follow the Lord God. What a glory for a nation to have a leader like that! And then in verse five, we find him appointing judges, judges which he then in verses six and seven reminded that they were judging for the LORD, not for man. He reminded them to be utterly impartial and to take no bribes. This was a king who understood that God is not a respecter of persons, and therefore we should not be either.

DO be consistently fair and impartial and "unbuyable." If money never sways God in His decisions, it should never sway us in our decisions either!

Personal Notes:

_____

_____

_____

_____

_____

_____

_____

_____

_____

_____

_____

_____

_____

_____

_____

_____

_____

_____

_____

_____

_____

_____

_____

_____

_____

_____

_____

_____

Devotion 10

King Jehoshaphat had things rolling along for God in Judah. But the devil never takes that kind of thing lying down…

2 Chronicles 20:1 *It came to pass after this also, that the children of Moab, and the children of Ammon, and with them other beside the Ammonites, came against Jehoshaphat to battle.* **2** *Then there came some that told Jehoshaphat, saying, There cometh a great multitude against thee from beyond the sea on this side Syria; and, behold, they be in Hazazontamar, which is Engedi.* **3** *And Jehoshaphat feared, and set himself to seek the LORD, and proclaimed a fast throughout all Judah.*

There are two things that thrill my soul as I read this. The first one is the obvious one: in a time of fear and trouble, King Jehoshaphat ran toward God instead of away from Him. That puts him in the minority; most people run away from God during times of fear and trouble.

But the second thing I find that thrills my soul is that in a day when there was no electronic surveillance, radar, or any other modern technology, some people saw trouble coming toward Jehoshaphat, and they came and told him. This puts them in the minority; most people "look the other way and mind their own business" in a situation like that.

Warning people of impending danger is never a pleasant thing; in fact, sometimes we do so and find ourselves having to plead, "Don't kill the messenger!" But whether they like it or not, people do need to be warned when they are heading for trouble or when trouble is heading for them. So DO be willing to be the messenger!

Personal Notes:

_____

_____

_____

_____

_____

_____

_____

_____

_____

_____

_____

_____

_____

_____

_____

_____

_____

_____

_____

_____

_____

_____

_____

_____

_____

Devotion 11

Moab and Ammon were coming to invade Judah. King Jehoshaphat, commander in chief of the army... held a prayer meeting with the nation. And his prayer is breathtaking.

2 Chronicles 20:5 *And Jehoshaphat stood in the congregation of Judah and Jerusalem, in the house of the LORD, before the new court,* **6** *And said, O LORD God of our fathers, art not thou God in heaven? and rulest not thou over all the kingdoms of the heathen? and in thine hand is there not power and might, so that none is able to withstand thee?* **7** *Art not thou our God, who didst drive out the inhabitants of this land before thy people Israel, and gavest it to the seed of Abraham thy friend for ever?* **8** *And they dwelt therein, and have built thee a sanctuary therein for thy name, saying,* **9** *If, when evil cometh upon us, as the sword, judgment, or pestilence, or famine, we stand before this house, and in thy presence, (for thy name is in this house,) and cry unto thee in our affliction, then thou wilt hear and help.* **10** *And now, behold, the children of Ammon and Moab and mount Seir, whom thou wouldest not let Israel invade, when they came out of the land of Egypt, but they turned from them, and destroyed them not;* **11** *Behold, I say, how they reward us, to come to cast us out of thy possession, which thou hast given us to inherit.* **12** *O our God, wilt thou not judge them? for we have no might against this great company that cometh against us; neither know we what to do: but our eyes are upon thee.*

In short, his prayer included accurate theology, accurate history, and accurate humility. Oh, that all prayers were so "Right!" When you pray, DO understand who God is, what He has already done, and just how much you need Him!

Personal Notes:

_____

_____

_____

_____

_____

_____

_____

_____

_____

_____

_____

_____

_____

_____

_____

_____

_____

_____

_____

_____

_____

_____

Devotion 12

After Jehoshaphat prayed his amazing prayer, God gave a prophet an immediate message in response.

2 Chronicles 20:14 *Then upon Jahaziel the son of Zechariah, the son of Benaiah, the son of Jeiel, the son of Mattaniah, a Levite of the sons of Asaph, came the Spirit of the LORD in the midst of the congregation;* **15** *And he said, Hearken ye, all Judah, and ye inhabitants of Jerusalem, and thou king Jehoshaphat, Thus saith the LORD unto you, Be not afraid nor dismayed by reason of this great multitude; for the battle is not yours, but God's.* **16** *To morrow go ye down against them: behold, they come up by the cliff of Ziz; and ye shall find them at the end of the brook, before the wilderness of Jeruel.* **17** *Ye shall not need to fight in this battle: set yourselves, stand ye still, and see the salvation of the LORD with you, O Judah and Jerusalem: fear not, nor be dismayed; to morrow go out against them: for the LORD will be with you.*

In this prophecy, we find one of the two common characteristics of true, God-given prophecy: specificity. The other one, by the way, is accuracy, and we will see that in the next devotion. But in this one notice that Jahaziel told everyone the very specific route the enemy was taking out of the many potential routes they could have taken. He then told them exactly where they would be on that route tomorrow when they went to confront them. He thirdly told them that they would not even need to fight in the battle.

DO cast a skeptical, disbelieving eye to the modern phony prophets and devilish astrologers whose "prophecies" are as generic as a fortune cookie; God can do much better than "you will be presented with an opportunity today!"

Personal Notes:

_____
_____
_____
_____
_____
_____
_____
_____
_____
_____
_____
_____
_____
_____
_____
_____
_____
_____
_____
_____
_____
_____
_____
_____

Devotion 13

King Jehoshaphat had an interesting "problem" to deal with. He was the commander in chief of the army but had just been informed that in the battle they were now marching toward, they would not need to fight! What, then, was he supposed to tell everyone to do? Fortunately, Jehoshaphat knew just the thing...

2 Chronicles 20:21 *And when he had consulted with the people, he appointed singers unto the LORD, and that should praise the beauty of holiness, as they went out before the army, and to say, Praise the LORD; for his mercy endureth for ever.* **22** *And when they began to sing and to praise, the LORD set ambushments against the children of Ammon, Moab, and mount Seir, which were come against Judah; and they were smitten.* **23** *For the children of Ammon and Moab stood up against the inhabitants of mount Seir, utterly to slay and destroy them: and when they had made an end of the inhabitants of Seir, every one helped to destroy another.* **24** *And when Judah came toward the watch tower in the wilderness, they looked unto the multitude, and, behold, they were dead bodies fallen to the earth, and none escaped.* **25** *And when Jehoshaphat and his people came to take away the spoil of them, they found among them in abundance both riches with the dead bodies, and precious jewels, which they stripped off for themselves, more than they could carry away: and they were three days in gathering of the spoil, it was so much.*

When the people gave God praise, God responded with power. And this pattern is still a good one for today! If you want God to move in power in your life, DO praise Him often and openly!

Personal Notes:

_____

_____

_____

_____

_____

_____

_____

_____

_____

_____

_____

_____

_____

_____

_____

_____

_____

_____

_____

_____

_____

_____

_____

_____

_____

Devotion 14

It is interesting to see how often people have a "hiccup" in their character that they never do fully eliminate. Godly Jehoshaphat was such a man. Early in his reign, he made the mistake of joining hearts, hands, and plans with wicked Ahab. And then near the end of his reign, we read this:

2 Chronicles 20:35 *And after this did Jehoshaphat king of Judah join himself with Ahaziah king of Israel, who did very wickedly:* **36** *And he joined himself with him to make ships to go to Tarshish: and they made the ships in Eziongeber.* **37** *Then Eliezer the son of Dodavah of Mareshah prophesied against Jehoshaphat, saying, Because thou hast joined thyself with Ahaziah, the LORD hath broken thy works. And the ships were broken, that they were not able to go to Tarshish.*

To paraphrase an old statement, "Fool me once, shame on you, but if I am such an idiot that I make the same mistake over and over again, shame on me." When Jehoshaphat joined with Ahab, he came a split second from losing his life in battle and did lose a substantial part of his army. Now he joins with wicked Ahaziah and loses an entire navy. Some people just never learn...

DO NOT be one of them. DO learn from your mistakes, especially in spiritual matters, and refrain from repeating, repeating, repeating them!

Personal Notes:

_____

_____

_____

_____

_____

_____

_____

_____

_____

_____

_____

_____

_____

_____

_____

_____

_____

_____

_____

_____

_____

_____

_____

_____

_____

Devotion 15

After godly Jehoshaphat, we find things in Judah taking a drastic turn for the worse:

2 Chronicles 21:1 *Now Jehoshaphat slept with his fathers, and was buried with his fathers in the city of David. And Jehoram his son reigned in his stead. 2 And he had brethren the sons of Jehoshaphat, Azariah, and Jehiel, and Zechariah, and Azariah, and Michael, and Shephatiah: all these were the sons of Jehoshaphat king of Israel. 3 And their father gave them great gifts of silver, and of gold, and of precious things, with fenced cities in Judah: but the kingdom gave he to Jehoram; because he was the firstborn. 4 Now when Jehoram was risen up to the kingdom of his father, he strengthened himself, and slew all his brethren with the sword, and divers also of the princes of Israel.*

This new king, Jehoram, was so very different from his father, so wicked, that he literally murdered most of his own family. What in the world went wrong? You will not have to look too far for the answer...

2 Chronicles 21:6 *And he walked in the way of the kings of Israel, like as did the house of Ahab: for he had the daughter of Ahab to wife: and he wrought that which was evil in the eyes of the LORD.*

His wickedness was specifically because of his wife. He married very, very wrong, and everyone around him paid the price for it.

If you are single, DO refuse to even have anything to do with a wicked potential mate, and if

you are raising children, teach this to them early and
often!

Personal Notes:

_____

_____

_____

_____

_____

_____

_____

_____

_____

_____

_____

_____

_____

_____

_____

_____

_____

_____

_____

_____

_____

_____

_____

_____

_____

_____

_____

_____

Devotion 16

Jehoram was going all out for evil. He murdered his family, he married the daughter of Ahab, and he was only getting started:

2 Chronicles 21:11 *Moreover he made high places in the mountains of Judah, and caused the inhabitants of Jerusalem to commit fornication, and compelled Judah thereto.*

Jehoram brought idolatry back to the land and, not content with being a likely fornicator himself, not even content with simply allowing and promoting fornication in the land, he "compelled Judah" to fornication. He actually pressured the entire nation into sexual sin. But if he thought that God would have to scramble and react to what he was doing, he was drastically, stunningly wrong:

2 Chronicles 21:12 *And there came a writing to him from Elijah the prophet, saying, Thus saith the LORD God of David thy father, Because thou hast not walked in the ways of Jehoshaphat thy father, nor in the ways of Asa king of Judah,* **13** *But hast walked in the way of the kings of Israel, and hast made Judah and the inhabitants of Jerusalem to go a whoring, like to the whoredoms of the house of Ahab, and also hast slain thy brethren of thy father's house, which were better than thyself:*

A letter? Why would a man as bold as Elijah send a letter? Well, mostly because had been in heaven for the past thirteen years...

Before Elijah ever left this world, God told him what was going to happen in the future and said, "Now write the man a letter..."

And he got every detail exactly right. DO remember how big our God is, and DO understand how perfect God's Word is. When God puts it in writing, He makes no mistakes!

Personal Notes:

_____

_____

_____

_____

_____

_____

_____

_____

_____

_____

_____

_____

_____

_____

_____

_____

_____

_____

_____

_____

_____

_____

Devotion 17

Jehoram, likely with trembling hands, was reading a letter that had been written by Elijah thirteen or more years earlier. That letter got every detail of Jehoram's sin correct, and he knew it. Therefore, he also knew that whatever the letter said would be one hundred percent accurate as well. What a kick in the gut it must have been, then, for him to read these words:

2 Chronicles 21:14 *Behold, with a great plague will the LORD smite thy people, and thy children, and thy wives, and all thy goods:* **15** *And thou shalt have great sickness by disease of thy bowels, until thy bowels fall out by reason of the sickness day by day.*

This gruesome description is almost certainly of a completely prolapsed rectum which then developed colorectal carcinoma, metastasized, and spread throughout his body. This man who was focused on sexual sin to such a degree that he compelled the nation to join in was judged by God with a disease that would make him too disgusting and ashamed to ever disrobe in front of anyone ever again.

This disease took his life. And the description given of people's reaction is jaw-dropping: verse twenty says, *"And he reigned in Jerusalem eight years, and departed without being desired."* That last phrase means that he was dead, no one cared, no one missed him, and no one would have brought him back if they could.

Ouch.

DO understand that promoting and pushing sin is a great way to gain temporary pleasure and permanent humiliation!

Personal Notes:

_____

_____

_____

_____

_____

_____

_____

_____

_____

_____

_____

_____

_____

_____

_____

_____

_____

_____

_____

_____

_____

_____

_____

_____

_____

_____

Devotion 18

After Jehoram's smelly and embarrassing death, the people of the land, showing incredibly poor discernment, put Ahaziah on the throne. He was an unmitigated disaster... and his mother could not have been more pleased.

2 Chronicles 22:2 *Forty and two years old was Ahaziah when he began to reign, and he reigned one year in Jerusalem. His mother's name also was Athaliah the daughter of Omri. 3 He also walked in the ways of the house of Ahab: for his mother was his counsellor to do wickedly.*

Let that last phrase bounce around your mind for just a moment, "his mother was his counselor to do wickedly." She did not just tolerate wickedness in her child as many modern mothers do; that would be bad enough. She went so far as to actually instruct him what to do wrong and how to do it. Talk about a horrible, horrible mother!

What can you possibly say about a person blessed with a child who intentionally leads that child into sin? How can we even begin to comprehend a parent that bad?

Fathers, mothers, determine now to be one hundred eighty degrees opposite from this woman. Determine now to instruct your children what to do right and how to do it. DO be the parents that make God happy He gave them children rather than the parents that make Him regret having given them children!

Personal Notes:

_____
_____
_____
_____
_____
_____
_____
_____
_____
_____
_____
_____
_____
_____
_____
_____
_____
_____
_____
_____
_____
_____
_____
_____
_____
_____
_____
_____
_____
_____

Devotion 19

Wicked and foolish Ahaziah did not last long at all on the throne, being slain pretty quickly by Jehu. But it is then that one of the most riveting dramas in all of human history began to play out.

2 Chronicles 22:10 *But when Athaliah the mother of Ahaziah saw that her son was dead, she arose and destroyed all the seed royal of the house of Judah.* **11** *But Jehoshabeath, the daughter of the king, took Joash the son of Ahaziah, and stole him from among the king's sons that were slain, and put him and his nurse in a bedchamber. So Jehoshabeath, the daughter of king Jehoram, the wife of Jehoiada the priest, (for she was the sister of Ahaziah,) hid him from Athaliah, so that she slew him not.* **12** *And he was with them hid in the house of God six years: and Athaliah reigned over the land.*

Reading this, you get a sense of the drama. But you do not really understand the full measure of it until you realize what was really at stake. Here is what Adam Clarke said of this:

"Nothing but the miraculous intervention of the Divine providence could have saved the line of David at this time and preserved the prophecy relative to the Messiah. The whole truth of that prophecy, and the salvation of the world, appeared to be now suspended on the brittle thread of the life of an infant of a year old, to destroy whom was the interest of the reigning power! But God can save by few as well as by many. He had purposed, and vain were the counter-exertions of earth and hell."

This was more than just a wicked woman killing people for power; this was Satan himself trying to keep Jesus from coming! And yet the very devil of hell could not stop one brave young woman named Jehoshabeath from rescuing one tiny baby and preserving the line of Christ.

DO understand that great futures for many are often secured by the brave and righteous actions of a single person in the present, and DO determine to always be that person!

Personal Notes:

_____

_____

_____

_____

_____

_____

_____

_____

_____

_____

_____

_____

_____

_____

_____

_____

_____

_____

_____

Devotion 20

For six years, wicked Athaliah, that murderous wretch, ruled as the queen. For six years, young Joash, the rightful king, grew unseen, hidden in the house of God. What must it have been like to try and explain to a very young boy that he was actually supposed to be the king and one day soon would be anointed as such and be embroiled in a power struggle for the throne?

In 2 Chronicles 23, that struggle took place, and it was an overwhelming victory. And it was not a politician that made it all happen, it was "a member of the clergy."

2 Chronicles 23:12 *Now when Athaliah heard the noise of the people running and praising the king, she came to the people into the house of the LORD:* **13** *And she looked, and, behold, the king stood at his pillar at the entering in, and the princes and the trumpets by the king: and all the people of the land rejoiced, and sounded with trumpets, also the singers with instruments of musick, and such as taught to sing praise. Then Athaliah rent her clothes, and said, Treason, Treason.* **14** *Then Jehoiada the priest brought out the captains of hundreds that were set over the host, and said unto them, Have her forth of the ranges: and whoso followeth her, let him be slain with the sword. For the priest said, Slay her not in the house of the LORD.* **15** *So they laid hands on her; and when she was come to the entering of the horse gate by the king's house, they slew her there.* **16** *And Jehoiada made a covenant between him, and between* *all the people, and between the king, that they should be the LORD'S people.*

We hear so often that Christians and churches and especially preachers should "keep their noses out of government." Jehoiada the priest would have disagreed.

DO be willing to do more than just quietly pray and worship; when God's people "keep their noses out of government," only crooked noses like Athaliah will be in government!

Personal Notes:

_____

_____

_____

_____

_____

_____

_____

_____

_____

_____

_____

_____

_____

_____

_____

_____

_____

_____

_____

_____

Devotion 21

After a couple of disastrous kings and one evil queen, Joash was, in most regards, a lengthy breath of fresh air:

2 Chronicles 24:1 *Joash was seven years old when he began to reign, and he reigned forty years in Jerusalem. His mother's name also was Zibiah of Beersheba.* **2** *And Joash did that which was right in the sight of the LORD all the days of Jehoiada the priest.*

We will see the latter failing of Joash in verses to come. But for now let us focus on the fact that Joash, the boy without a father, the boy whose own grandmother tried to murder him, had a father figure to lean on and did so. Jehoiada the priest stepped in and filled the gap, and the young boy received all of the guidance he needed to do right and fulfill his potential for God.

Those who have ever had someone step in as a father or mother figure know how precious and powerful this is!

If you have a gap of leadership and influence that needs to be filled in your life, you would be wise to pray and seek it out. A godly mentor is worth more than a mountain of gold! And if you see someone who needs a godly mentor, you should be willing, and able, and forward to be what they need.

DO seek a mentor if you need one, and DO be a mentor to others who need one!

Personal Notes:

Devotion 22

Joash was on the throne, a bit of time had passed, and he set his sights on repairing the damage that his grandmother, Athaliah, had done to the house of God.

2 Chronicles 24:4 *And it came to pass after this, that Joash was minded to repair the house of the LORD.*

If you are surprised by a king, a politician, being interested in repairing the house of God, you will be even more surprised by the clergy's reaction to that suggestion:

2 Chronicles 24:5 *And he gathered together the priests and the Levites, and said to them, Go out unto the cities of Judah, and gather of all Israel money to repair the house of your God from year to year, and see that ye hasten the matter. Howbeit the Levites hastened it not.*

The king: "Hurry up with this repair work on the house of God, priests!"

The priests: "Nope, not in a hurry."

Mind you, we are not told they were opposed to the idea; they were simply apathetic to it...

Apathy has always been a far greater danger to the house of God and the work of God than active opposition. Far more metal rusts than is beaten away with a sledgehammer!

DO go beyond just "not being opposed to the work of God;" get in there and get busy at it!

Personal Notes:

_____
_____
_____
_____
_____
_____
_____
_____
_____
_____
_____
_____
_____
_____
_____
_____
_____
_____
_____
_____
_____
_____
_____
_____
_____
_____
_____

Devotion 23

King Joash found himself with a surprising problem. Jehoiada the priest, the man so very interested in the political life of the nation that he had wicked queen Athaliah assassinated and put young Joash on the throne, turned out to be lazy and unconcerned when it came to repairing the house of God and the spiritual life of the nation. And the priests were right there with him in that apathy.

So Joash the king took matters into his own hands:

2 Chronicles 24:6 *And the king called for Jehoiada the chief, and said unto him, Why hast thou not required of the Levites to bring in out of Judah and out of Jerusalem the collection, according to the commandment of Moses the servant of the LORD, and of the congregation of Israel, for the tabernacle of witness?* **7** *For the sons of Athaliah, that wicked woman, had broken up the house of God; and also all the dedicated things of the house of the LORD did they bestow upon Baalim.* **8** *And at the king's commandment they made a chest, and set it without at the gate of the house of the LORD.* **9** *And they made a proclamation through Judah and Jerusalem, to bring in to the LORD the collection that Moses the servant of God laid upon Israel in the wilderness.* **10** *And all the princes and all the people rejoiced, and brought in, and cast into the chest, until they had made an end.*

Verse ten is striking to me. It was not the priests that rejoiced at the giving which would repair the house of God; it was the princes (the political class) and the people (the citizens). Something is seriously wrong and right with that picture!

DO rejoice in any progress at the house of God, especially if anyone is actually looking to you as any type of spiritual leader!

Personal Notes:

_____

_____

_____

_____

_____

_____

_____

_____

_____

_____

_____

_____

_____

_____

_____

_____

_____

_____

_____

_____

_____

_____

_____

Devotion 24

Jehoiada, despite his initial slowness to repair the house of God, was still one of the greatest figures in Jewish history. In fact, he and his family literally rescued not just King Joash but the line of David itself, and therefore, the line of Jesus our Messiah! It is understandable, then, that we read these words concerning his death and burial:

2 Chronicles 24:15 *But Jehoiada waxed old, and was full of days when he died; an hundred and thirty years old was he when he died.* **16** *And they buried him in the city of David among the kings, because he had done good in Israel, both toward God, and toward his house.*

This man was a priest, not a king. And yet he was buried among the kings, something that under normal circumstances he would have been barred from. What a testimony of gratitude to a legitimate, real-life hero!

DO understand that you are capable of doing great things for God, perhaps greater than you or anyone else around you even realizes!

Personal Notes:

_____
_____
_____
_____
_____
_____
_____
_____
_____
_____
_____
_____
_____
_____
_____
_____
_____
_____
_____
_____
_____
_____
_____
_____
_____
_____
_____
_____

Devotion 25

Joash was, officially, the king. But it was Jehoiada the priest who was the "living set of convictions" for the king. And that is a bad thing...

2 Chronicles 24:17 *Now after the death of Jehoiada came the princes of Judah, and made obeisance to the king. Then the king hearkened unto them.* **18** *And they left the house of the LORD God of their fathers, and served groves and idols: and wrath came upon Judah and Jerusalem for this their trespass.*

When Jehoiada was alive, King Joash did right because it is what Jehoiada demanded. But when Jehoiada was dead, King Joash did wrong because it is what the princes of Judah demanded. In other words, Joash had no real convictions at all; he simply conformed to whatever the prevailing pressure around him was.

The man had the crown, but he had no convictions.

No person is more useless than a person who bows to every wind that blows. DO get in the Bible, study and learn it, develop unshakable convictions based upon it, and then never bow to any contrary pressure!

Personal Notes:

Devotion 26

God was not simply going to allow the princes of Judah and pliable King Joash to forsake God and follow idols. So he sent a man to the king to rebuke him. But not just any man, no, not by a long shot...

2 Chronicles 24:19 *Yet he sent prophets to them, to bring them again unto the LORD; and they testified against them: but they would not give ear.* **20** *And the Spirit of God came upon Zechariah the son of Jehoiada the priest, which stood above the people, and said unto them, Thus saith God, Why transgress ye the commandments of the LORD, that ye cannot prosper? because ye have forsaken the LORD, he hath also forsaken you.*

Zechariah... the son of Jehoiada the priest...

God sent King Joash the son of the man who saved his life as a baby, hid him for six years, risked his life to put him on the throne, and then guided him for years. Joash owed Jehoiada everything. But look at how he repaid that kindness:

2 Chronicles 24:21 *And they conspired against him, and stoned him with stones at the commandment of the king in the court of the house of the LORD.* **22** *Thus Joash the king remembered not the kindness which Jehoiada his father had done to him, but slew his son. And when he died, he said, The LORD look upon it, and require it.*

God have mercy. He killed Jehoiada's son! How wicked and ungrateful!

DO be better than that. When people have done good to you, never turn around and repay them with horrible unkindness!

Personal Notes:

_____

_____

_____

_____

_____

_____

_____

_____

_____

_____

_____

_____

_____

_____

_____

_____

_____

_____

_____

_____

_____

_____

_____

Devotion 27

When Joash murdered the son of the man to whom he owed everything, God would not let it pass by unaddressed.

2 Chronicles 24:23 *And it came to pass at the end of the year, that the host of Syria came up against him: and they came to Judah and Jerusalem, and destroyed all the princes of the people from among the people, and sent all the spoil of them unto the king of Damascus.* **24** *For the army of the Syrians came with a small company of men, and the LORD delivered a very great host into their hand, because they had forsaken the LORD God of their fathers. So they executed judgment against Joash.* **25** *And when they were departed from him, (for they left him in great diseases,) his own servants conspired against him for the blood of the sons of Jehoiada the priest, and slew him on his bed, and he died...*

We noted earlier that Jehoiada the priest was buried among the kings. And now, completing the irony, we read this of King Joash at the end of verse twenty-six, *"and they buried him in the city of David, but they buried him not in the sepulchres of the kings."*

A "mere citizen" was buried among the kings, and a king was buried among mere citizens. This was God's rather eloquent way of reminding us that where we end up is not determined by where we start but by the decisions we make along the way!

Both for the sake of time and the sake of eternity, DO make all the right decisions. And "all the right decisions" can be summed up in just two overarching decisions. One, get save, and two, live right!

Personal Notes:

_____

_____

_____

_____

_____

_____

_____

_____

_____

_____

_____

_____

_____

_____

_____

_____

_____

_____

_____

_____

_____

_____

_____

_____

_____

_____

_____

_____

Devotion 28

We know from verse twenty-five that King Joash's own servants were the ones who killed him. In the next verse we are given their names and their backgrounds:

2 Chronicles 24:26 *And these are they that conspired against him; Zabad the son of Shimeath an Ammonitess, and Jehozabad the son of Shimrith a Moabitess.*

Zabad and Jehozabad were foreigners, both from nations that had for a very long time been enemies of God and of Israel. And look at the access they were given; verse twenty-five tells us that they killed the king on his own bed! This was, to put it mildly, not prudent at all on the part of Joash. And it would be a few years before the situation was remedied... but it was ultimately remedied.

2 Chronicles 25:1 *Amaziah was twenty and five years old when he began to reign, and he reigned twenty and nine years in Jerusalem. And his mother's name was Jehoaddan of Jerusalem.* **2** *And he did that which was right in the sight of the LORD, but not with a perfect heart.* **3** *Now it came to pass, when the kingdom was established to him, that he slew his servants that had killed the king his father.*

Joash made a horrible mistake, and yet, it was a mistake very common to kings of those ages. It was utterly normal for them to have foreigners as their valets and trusted confidants. But Amaziah, his son, put those men to death once he had the power to do so. The fact that his father had made a mistake was not regarded by him as a good reason to continue in that mistake himself.

We all have guides in our lives: parents, pastors, teachers, and many more. But all of them have at least one thing in common: they are all human and, therefore, have the potential to make mistakes.

DO be willing to follow the examples of your guides when those examples are good and sensible and right. But DO be equally willing to forsake the example of your guides when those examples are not good and insensible and not right! Remember that all who come before us are merely guides, not gods.

Personal Notes:

_____

_____

_____

_____

_____

_____

_____

_____

_____

_____

_____

_____

_____

_____

_____

_____

_____

_____

Devotion 29

Verse two tells us that Amaziah *"did that which was right in the sight of the LORD, but not with a perfect heart."* At that point, you can almost hear the ominous music beginning to play and the narrator's voice in the background saying, "But storm clouds were gathering overhead..."

In the next few verses, the king determined to go to war. He gathered his own forces and then made the mistake of hiring, for an exorbitant sum, 100,000 soldiers from Israel, the northern kingdom. A prophet of God told him to send them back, or God would make sure they lost. He did so and decisively won the battle without them. But then we read this:

2 Chronicles 25:14 *Now it came to pass, after that Amaziah was come from the slaughter of the Edomites, that he brought the gods of the children of Seir [the Edomites], and set them up to be his gods, and bowed down himself before them, and burned incense unto them.*

This was forever the most boneheaded mistake Jewish kings consistently made. They defeated their enemies and their enemies' pitiful little gods... and then brought those pitiful little defeated gods home to worship. If those "gods" were not able to help the people that they just defeated, why would the Jewish kings think that they could help them? Why would you worship a god that you defeated on the battlefield and carried home like a souvenir from a foreign trinket shop?

I can supply you with that answer. This was not about success; it was about sensuality. The real God demanded holy and righteous living from His people. The gods they were defeating left and right had temple prostitutes and encouraged every wicked indulgence of the flesh.

It is very much like the fake "Jesus" that modern "woke" Christianity has invented today, for whom no sexual activity is off-limits and no matter how deviant is to be celebrated. The eventual defeat from following that false god is just as inevitable as the defeat that occurred every time Israel did it.

DO follow and worship only the real God who can be recognized by His expectations of holiness from those who follow Him!

Personal Notes:

_____

_____

_____

_____

_____

_____

_____

_____

_____

_____

_____

_____

_____

_____

Devotion 30

God was not going to let King Amaziah get by with worshipping the false gods that had just recently been defeated by the one true God.

2 Chronicles 25:15 *Wherefore the anger of the LORD was kindled against Amaziah, and he sent unto him a prophet, which said unto him, Why hast thou sought after the gods of the people, which could not deliver their own people out of thine hand?*

This was a logical, sensible question. It should have been enough to snap the king out of his stupor and get him to recognize what an idiot he was being. But, sadly, an idiot with power is much harder to ever get through to than any average idiot...

2 Chronicles 25:16 *And it came to pass, as he talked with him, that the king said unto him, Art thou made of the king's counsel? forbear; why shouldest thou be smitten? Then the prophet forbare, and said, I know that God hath determined to destroy thee, because thou hast done this, and hast not hearkened unto my counsel.*

A good paraphrase of what this proud king said is, "How dare you presume to give me counsel without me asking for it? Who do you think you are?" He then proceeded to demand that the prophet fall silent, threatening to smite him and doubtless kill him if he did not. So this unnamed prophet stopped giving his counsel and instead simply informed the king that it no longer even mattered and that God was going to kill him.

It puts one very much in mind of an old commercial that said, "We can do this the easy way, or we can do this the hard way..."

Humbly taking godly counsel is the easy way. Pridefully refusing godly counsel and then suffering ruin because of that is the hard way. DO everything the easy way!

Personal Notes:

_____

_____

_____

_____

_____

_____

_____

_____

_____

_____

_____

_____

_____

_____

_____

_____

_____

_____

_____

_____

_____

_____

_____

Devotion 31

Amaziah had defeated the Edomites and then foolishly taken their gods home to worship. A prophet of God had confronted him about that transgression, and the king quickly shut him down. But though the messenger of God can be silenced, the God of the messenger cannot...

2 Chronicles 25:17 *Then Amaziah king of Judah took advice, and sent to Joash, the son of Jehoahaz, the son of Jehu, king of Israel, saying, Come, let us see one another in the face.* **18** *And Joash king of Israel sent to Amaziah king of Judah, saying, The thistle that was in Lebanon sent to the cedar that was in Lebanon, saying, Give thy daughter to my son to wife: and there passed by a wild beast that was in Lebanon, and trode down the thistle.* **19** *Thou sayest, Lo, thou hast smitten the Edomites; and thine heart lifteth thee up to boast: abide now at home; why shouldest thou meddle to thine hurt, that thou shouldest fall, even thou, and Judah with thee?* **20** *But Amaziah would not hear; for it came of God, that he might deliver them into the hand of their enemies, because they sought after the gods of Edom.*

Having beaten a fairly small force of the Edomites, Amaziah, king of Judah, was lifted up in pride and imagined that he was powerful enough to defeat neighboring Israel. He sent to the king of Israel and announced his intention to do so, and the king of Israel sent back a fable as a message. The moral of the fable was that Amaziah was an insignificant thistle who now imagine himself to be a cedar and that thinking that way was going to get him stomped into the ground.

But even more interesting than the fable is the fact that the wicked king of Israel did not want to see neighboring Judah fall. The two kingdoms had once been one, and even evil Joash was willing to respect that.

It is good that we show a certain measure of respect for the bonds of the past. None of us got to where we are out of nowhere; we are all standing on the foundation of previous generations. This generation seems particularly intent on destroying and disavowing all past foundations and bonds; DO be smart enough not to go along with them!

Personal Notes:

_____
_____
_____
_____
_____
_____
_____
_____
_____
_____
_____
_____
_____
_____
_____

Devotion 32

Amaziah's mind was made up; he was going to war against Israel, no matter what any prophet or king or even God Himself had to say. I bet you can guess how well that went for him before you even read the text...

2 Chronicles 25:21 *So Joash the king of Israel went up; and they saw one another in the face, both he and Amaziah king of Judah, at Bethshemesh, which belongeth to Judah. 22 And Judah was put to the worse before Israel, and they fled every man to his tent. 23 And Joash the king of Israel took Amaziah king of Judah, the son of Joash, the son of Jehoahaz, at Bethshemesh, and brought him to Jerusalem, and brake down the wall of Jerusalem from the gate of Ephraim to the corner gate, four hundred cubits. 24 And he took all the gold and the silver, and all the vessels that were found in the house of God with Obededom, and the treasures of the king's house, the hostages also, and returned to Samaria.*

Amaziah was whipped on the battlefield. But that was just the beginning of his humiliation. King Joash of Israel dragged him back to his own capital city, Jerusalem, in front of his own people, and proceeded to tear down six hundred feet of the wall of Jerusalem in front of everyone. Then he took all the gold and silver from the house of God and from the king's treasuries, then he took hostages, and took everything and everyone back to his own capital city of Samaria, leaving Amaziah utterly humiliated and bankrupt before his own nation.

As we would say it in modern vernacular, "Play stupid games, win stupid prizes."

DO be in the habit of doing the opposite of what your pride tells you that you should do; no one ever honestly says, "I am so glad I followed my pride; that really went well!"

Personal Notes:

_____

_____

_____

_____

_____

_____

_____

_____

_____

_____

_____

_____

_____

_____

_____

_____

_____

_____

_____

_____

_____

_____

Devotion 33

King Amaziah of Judah, who started off so well, was eventually murdered by his own people because of the disaster he created by turning away from the LORD later in his life. His son, though, was going to be one of the bright spots in Judah's history.

2 Chronicles 26:1 *Then all the people of Judah took Uzziah, who was sixteen years old, and made him king in the room of his father Amaziah.* **2** *He built Eloth, and restored it to Judah, after that the king slept with his fathers.* **3** *Sixteen years old was Uzziah when he began to reign, and he reigned fifty and two years in Jerusalem. His mother's name also was Jecoliah of Jerusalem.* **4** *And he did that which was right in the sight of the LORD, according to all that his father Amaziah did.* **5** *And he sought God in the days of Zechariah, who had understanding in the visions of God: and as long as he sought the LORD, God made him to prosper.*

Of all the wonderful things said here about Uzziah, that last phrase in verse five is one that most catches my attention: *"as long as he sought the LORD, God made him to prosper."* This is clearly an either/or statement as well as a statement verifying the free will of man. Uzziah had a choice whether to seek God or not, and for most of his life, he chose to seek Him. And as long as he chose to seek God, God made him to prosper.

God does not make anyone seek Him, nor does He keep anyone from seeking Him. He allows everyone the free will to seek Him or not, and He responds accordingly. God put it this way to Jeremiah in **Jeremiah 29:13** *And ye shall seek me, and find me, when ye shall search for me with all your heart.*

Whether God ever made us to prosper or not by our seeking of Him, seeking Him would still be the right thing to do. But DO be encouraged by the fact that in ways too numerous to count, God still prospers those who seek Him!

Personal Notes:

_____

_____

_____

_____

_____

_____

_____

_____

_____

_____

_____

_____

_____

_____

_____

_____

_____

_____

_____

_____

_____

_____

Devotion 34

As we continue reading the account of King Uzziah, we quickly learn that the man was not just a battler; he was also a builder.

2 Chronicles 26:6 *And he went forth and warred against the Philistines, and brake down the wall of Gath, and the wall of Jabneh, and the wall of Ashdod, and built cities about Ashdod, and among the Philistines.* **7** *And God helped him against the Philistines, and against the Arabians that dwelt in Gurbaal, and the Mehunims.* **8** *And the Ammonites gave gifts to Uzziah: and his name spread abroad even to the entering in of Egypt; for he strengthened himself exceedingly.* **9** *Moreover Uzziah built towers in Jerusalem at the corner gate, and at the valley gate, and at the turning of the wall, and fortified them.* **10** *Also he built towers in the desert, and digged many wells: for he had much cattle, both in the low country, and in the plains: husbandmen also, and vine dressers in the mountains, and in Carmel: for he loved husbandry.*

Cities in Philistine territory. Towers in Jerusalem. Towers in the desert. Multiple wells dug. Vineyards planted all over the place. Uzziah spent a great deal of his time building things that would outlast him and be a blessing to future generations. Anyone can tear things down. An idiot with a sledgehammer and an IQ of four can tear something down. But people with wisdom and foresight do not spend all their time in demolition; they think of the future and build things that matter.

Our country is seeing a lot of sledgehammer-wielding demolitionists these days, people who are intent on tearing down what others built before them. But what are they building? What have they built? If all a person or organization does is demolition, he or they are not worthy of being followed.

DO be a builder!

Personal Notes:

_____

_____

_____

_____

_____

_____

_____

_____

_____

_____

_____

_____

_____

_____

_____

_____

_____

_____

_____

_____

Devotion 35

King Uzziah, among other accomplishments, was a man of technology, especially in weaponry.

2 Chronicles 26:11 *Moreover Uzziah had an host of fighting men, that went out to war by bands, according to the number of their account by the hand of Jeiel the scribe and Maaseiah the ruler, under the hand of Hananiah, one of the king's captains.* **12** *The whole number of the chief of the fathers of the mighty men of valour were two thousand and six hundred.* **13** *And under their hand was an army, three hundred thousand and seven thousand and five hundred, that made war with mighty power, to help the king against the enemy.* **14** *And Uzziah prepared for them throughout all the host shields, and spears, and helmets, and habergeons, and bows, and slings to cast stones.* **15** *And he made in Jerusalem engines, invented by cunning men, to be on the towers and upon the bulwarks, to shoot arrows and great stones withal. And his name spread far abroad; for he was marvellously helped, till he was strong.*

When we read these words, we get an accurate picture in our mind of ancient machines on great stone walls catapulting rocks at the enemy and shooting thousands of arrows at a time. We also tend to yawn at those things because they seem so "old-fashioned" to us. We have seen movies of many ancient cities and empires doing these very things.

But the significant thing to note here is that Uzziah and Judah were roughly eight hundred years ahead of their time in so doing! Little wonder, then, that the last thing we read in verse fifteen is, *"for he was marvellously helped, till he was strong."*

Being "late to the party" lends itself to weakness, not strength. That being the case, DO, in everything, be as wise and up-to-date and cutting-edge as you can righteously be!

Personal Notes:

_____

_____

_____

_____

_____

_____

_____

_____

_____

_____

_____

_____

_____

_____

_____

_____

_____

_____

_____

_____

_____

_____

_____

Devotion 36

In a scene so repetitive that it is utterly heartbreaking, King Uzziah of Judah eventually took a turn for the worse...

2 Chronicles 26:16 *But when he was strong, his heart was lifted up to his destruction: for he transgressed against the LORD his God, and went into the temple of the LORD to burn incense upon the altar of incense.*

So often when we read of people transgressing against the Lord, we are warned of things like fornication and adultery and homosexuality. But in this case, the transgression was "worship!" Uzziah was not killing anyone or stealing anything or being perverted; he just wanted to burn incense to the Lord on the altar of incense. So what's the big deal? The big deal is that God ordained the kings to come from the tribe of Judah and the priests to come from the tribe of Levi. And only the priests, with no exceptions whatsoever, were allowed into the holy place to perform the functions of worship. What they could do righteously could only be done unrighteously by others. Some sins are a matter of what; some sins are a matter of who. Anything we do that God has designated only for others to do is a sin, specifically the sin of rebellion. This was the exact same sin that King Saul, the very first king of Israel, engaged in.

We really need to understand that since God is God, He has the right to reserve whatever tasks and positions He chooses to whomever He chooses. Whether it be the pastorate and the deaconship that he has reserved specifically to men or the fact that the qualifications of the ministry in 1 Timothy 3 actually eliminate a great many men, either God gets to be God in this, or we get to be God in this.

And we do not get to be God.

DO let God be God; if He would not bow to Uzziah in this (and we will see in the next devotion that He would not), He most certainly will not bow to us!

Personal Notes:

_____

_____

_____

_____

_____

_____

_____

_____

_____

_____

_____

_____

_____

_____

_____

_____

_____

_____

_____

_____

Devotion 37

King Uzziah had barged into the Temple, grabbed the golden censer, and started trying to offer incense to God. But only priests, sons of Aaron, were allowed to do so. And that made a "good thing" (serving God) a bad thing. A horrible thing, in fact. And the real priests were not simply going to meekly stand by and watch as the most powerful man in the nation defied God and defiled His house.

2 Chronicles 26:17 *And Azariah the priest went in after him, and with him fourscore priests of the LORD, that were valiant men:* **18** *And they withstood Uzziah the king, and said unto him, It appertaineth not unto thee, Uzziah, to burn incense unto the LORD, but to the priests the sons of Aaron, that are consecrated to burn incense: go out of the sanctuary; for thou hast trespassed; neither shall it be for thine honour from the LORD God.*

This was a very good and very early proper application of the concept of "separation of church and state." Normally that phrase (which is not found in the Constitution, by the way) is used to mean that believers need to stay out of government and governmental issues. But these brave priests showed that what such a concept really means is that we must never allow the government to interfere with the church! And if need be, we need to be willing to get positively belligerent about that.

These men told the king, of all people, to "get out."

DO understand that while believers throughout Scripture are seen as being involved in politics and political matters, they are also equally seen as refusing to let politicians tell them what to do when it comes to the house of God. The day we give that principle up is the day we guarantee that the church, if it even survives, will at best be just a wholly owned and operated subsidiary of government, a religious political prostitute.

Personal Notes:

_____

_____

_____

_____

_____

_____

_____

_____

_____

_____

_____

_____

_____

_____

_____

_____

_____

_____

_____

_____

_____

Devotion 38

When the priests stood against King Uzziah's trespassing, he became positively irate. But his anger was going to be very short-lived. Not because he felt guilty, but because One much mightier that he suddenly weighed in on the situation in the most dramatic of ways:

2 Chronicles 26:19 *Then Uzziah was wroth, and had a censer in his hand to burn incense: and while he was wroth with the priests, the leprosy even rose up in his forehead before the priests in the house of the LORD, from beside the incense altar.* **20** *And Azariah the chief priest, and all the priests, looked upon him, and, behold, he was leprous in his forehead, and they thrust him out from thence; yea, himself hasted also to go out, because the LORD had smitten him.* **21** *And Uzziah the king was a leper unto the day of his death, and dwelt in a several house, being a leper; for he was cut off from the house of the LORD: and Jotham his son was over the king's house, judging the people of the land.*

There was no more feared and abhorred thing in all the world in those days than leprosy. It was an incurable death sentence meted out over the course of many painful, loathsome years. God smote Uzziah with such sudden and visible leprosy that it became a race to see if he could run out of the Temple before the priests threw him out. He was now an outcast from all of society, cut off from human contact until the day he died. His son had to step in and rule while he literally rotted away.

And none of it was necessary. This was not simply a random sickness; it was a direct judgment.

DO understand that God is still God, and still holy, and still very much in charge. Wise people walk with Him, not contrary to Him!

Personal Notes:

_____

_____

_____

_____

_____

_____

_____

_____

_____

_____

_____

_____

_____

_____

_____

_____

_____

_____

_____

_____

_____

_____

_____

Devotion 39

Jotham would be one of the very rare kings in Judah's history of which no sin whatsoever is mentioned. And yet, as his account begins, we do find something that, if properly understood, is a bit sad.

2 Chronicles 27:1 *Jotham was twenty and five years old when he began to reign, and he reigned sixteen years in Jerusalem. His mother's name also was Jerushah, the daughter of Zadok. **2** And he did that which was right in the sight of the LORD, according to all that his father Uzziah did: howbeit he entered not into the temple of the LORD. And the people did yet corruptly.*

Uzziah, his father, had, except for one huge error later in life, been a good and godly king. His one huge error, of course, was going into the Temple and trying to intrude into the priesthood. So when 2 Chronicles 27 tells us that Jotham *"did that which was right in the sight of the LORD, according to all that his father Uzziah did,"* and then says, *"howbeit he entered not into the temple of the LORD,"* many commentators view this as a good thing, believing it to mean that he did not try to intrude into the priesthood as his father had done.

But this verse does not say that he did not try to offer incense as his father had done; it simply says that he did not even enter into the house of the LORD at all. Every Jewish male was supposed to be going to the Temple to worship multiple times a year. But these words seem clearly to tell us that he did not do so. Later on in the text, we find that he did worship;

in fact, he "prepared his ways before the LORD his God" according to verse six. But it seems as if the shame of what his father had done there, or perhaps the fear of what had happened to his father, kept him from ever going to the house of God again. Little wonder, then, that while he did right personally and privately, the nation around him devolved into wickedness and idolatry.

DO refuse to ever get out of church over some hurt or fear from the past. Others are always watching, and your simple choice to just worship privately will lead many of them so far afield as to sin openly!

Personal Notes:

_____

_____

_____

_____

_____

_____

_____

_____

_____

_____

_____

_____

_____

_____

_____

_____

_____

_____

Devotion 40

After reigning for sixteen years, good king Jotham died at forty-one years of age. His son, Ahaz, took the throne. And Ahaz utterly ignored the good examples of his father and grandfather and became one of the worst kings Judah would ever know.

2 Chronicles 28:1 *Ahaz was twenty years old when he began to reign, and he reigned sixteen years in Jerusalem: but he did not that which was right in the sight of the LORD, like David his father:* **2** *For he walked in the ways of the kings of Israel, and made also molten images for Baalim.* **3** *Moreover he burnt incense in the valley of the son of Hinnom, and burnt his children in the fire, after the abominations of the heathen whom the LORD had cast out before the children of Israel.* **4** *He sacrificed also and burnt incense in the high places, and on the hills, and under every green tree.*

These verses show us a picture of a king who was not simply moderately wicked, but utterly, thoroughly, aggressively, enthusiastically wicked. He went so far as to sacrifice some of his own babies to death in his idolatrous rituals, burning them in the fire. This was forever the very worst abomination of the heathens and the main thing that God despised in them and told His people to avoid.

There is simply no greater wickedness than putting innocent babies to death. And yet how many today still bow at the altar of Planned Parenthood, give homage to goddess Margaret Sanger, and utter their favorite phrases of worship such as "It's a woman's right to choose" and "My body, my choice"?

DO understand that God has never changed His mind on this, nor is He impressed that "business" has moved from the field to the office complex and from the stone hand of Moloch to the sterilized table of an abortion clinic.

Personal Notes:

_____

_____

_____

_____

_____

_____

_____

_____

_____

_____

_____

_____

_____

_____

_____

_____

_____

_____

_____

_____

_____

_____

_____

_____

Devotion 41

God's judgment against Ahaz and Judah for their horrible wickedness was going to be swift and severe:

2 Chronicles 28:5 *Wherefore the LORD his God delivered him into the hand of the king of Syria; and they smote him, and carried away a great multitude of them captives, and brought them to Damascus. And he was also delivered into the hand of the king of Israel, who smote him with a great slaughter.* **6** *For Pekah the son of Remaliah slew in Judah an hundred and twenty thousand in one day, which were all valiant men; because they had forsaken the LORD God of their fathers.* **7** *And Zichri, a mighty man of Ephraim, slew Maaseiah the king's son, and Azrikam the governor of the house, and Elkanah that was next to the king.* **8** *And the children of Israel carried away captive of their brethren two hundred thousand, women, sons, and daughters, and took also away much spoil from them, and brought the spoil to Samaria.*

Two separate attacks from two separate kingdoms leveled Judah. Syria struck them, and then Israel did as well. Just in the attack from Israel, Judah lost 120,000 men as well as a prince, a governor of the king's house, and the king's main advisor. They also had 200,000 women and children hauled away as captives and pretty much anything of value that was not nailed down.

This was a crushing blow to Judah. And it was their sin that brought them so low, not simply random chance. Their wickedness brought blisterings when they could have had blessings. And while we clearly see the judgment of God in all of this, in the next section of verses we will also see His amazing mercy.

For now, though, DO reflect on your own life and ask yourself whether you want God's blessings or God's blisterings!

Personal Notes:

_____

_____

_____

_____

_____

_____

_____

_____

_____

_____

_____

_____

_____

_____

_____

_____

_____

_____

_____

_____

_____

_____

Devotion 42

God had granted Israel a crushing victory over Judah because of Judah's sin. But to say that Israel took things way too far would be an understatement. And the most heinous thing they did was take 200,000 women and children captive back to their homeland. Israel just ignored that they were literally related to everyone from Judah and also that the women and children were innocent victims who had done nothing. Fortunately, there were some voices in Israel brave enough to stand up against their own leadership and call them out on this wickedness.

2 Chronicles 28:9 *But a prophet of the LORD was there, whose name was Oded: and he went out before the host that came to Samaria, and said unto them, Behold, because the LORD God of your fathers was wroth with Judah, he hath delivered them into your hand, and ye have slain them in a rage that reacheth up unto heaven.* **10** *And now ye purpose to keep under the children of Judah and Jerusalem for bondmen and bondwomen unto you: but are there not with you, even with you, sins against the LORD your God?* **11** *Now hear me therefore, and deliver the captives again, which ye have taken captive of your brethren: for the fierce wrath of the LORD is upon you.* **12** *Then certain of the heads of the children of Ephraim, Azariah the son of Johanan, Berechiah the son of Meshillemoth, and Jehizkiah the son of Shallum, and Amasa the son of Hadlai, stood up against them that came from the war,* **13** *And said unto them, Ye shall not bring in the captives hither:*

for whereas we have offended against the LORD already, ye intend to add more to our sins and to our trespass: for our trespass is great, and there is fierce wrath against Israel.

This is the only place in the Bible that we read about this particular man, Oded the prophet. He is two hundred years removed from an earlier prophet by that name in 2 Chronicles 15. This one brave soul stood up against an entire army—and as a result, four prominent princes stood up and put their foot down on the issue as well. It is amazing the impact one person can have when they are brave enough to stand up for what is right.

DO be willing to stand for right, even if you fear you may have to do so alone, because others may simply be waiting for someone else to take the lead!

Personal Notes:

_____

_____

_____

_____

_____

_____

_____

_____

_____

_____

_____

_____

_____

Devotion 43

Oded and the four princes of Israel told the army that they could not bring the captives into Samaria and that they had to send them back. But then came the most beautifully shocking part of all:

2 Chronicles 28:14 *So the armed men left the captives and the spoil before the princes and all the congregation.* **15** *And the men which were expressed by name rose up, and took the captives, and with the spoil clothed all that were naked among them, and arrayed them, and shod them, and gave them to eat and to drink, and anointed them, and carried all the feeble of them upon asses, and brought them to Jericho, the city of palm trees, to their brethren: then they returned to Samaria.*

I do not know of another instance like this in the history of the world. Israel took the spoil they brought home from the war, their "payday," and used it to clothe, feed, and tend to the wounds of their captives. Then they took all of the captives which they had intended to use as slaves and concubines and safely brought them back home to where they had taken them from.

And they did not even know God. They had abandoned Him generations ago in favor of Jeroboam's golden calves.

If the lost, wicked, heathen world can be so kind, surely, we who know Christ can as well! Each day that we live, we do so in a world of people who could desperately use such kindness; so DO be one who gives it!

Personal Notes:

_____
_____
_____
_____
_____
_____
_____
_____
_____
_____
_____
_____
_____
_____
_____
_____
_____
_____
_____
_____
_____
_____
_____
_____
_____
_____
_____
_____
_____

Devotion 44

The captives were back home in Judah after being returned by Israel. But things in Judah were still just as bad as ever, thanks to wicked King Ahaz.

2 Chronicles 28:16 *At that time did king Ahaz send unto the kings of Assyria to help him.* **17** *For again the Edomites had come and smitten Judah, and carried away captives.* **18** *The Philistines also had invaded the cities of the low country, and of the south of Judah, and had taken Bethshemesh, and Ajalon, and Gederoth, and Shocho with the villages thereof, and Timnah with the villages thereof, Gimzo also and the villages thereof: and they dwelt there.* **19** *For the LORD brought Judah low because of Ahaz king of Israel; for he made Judah naked, and transgressed sore against the LORD.*

Not learning the lessons of the judgment that recently fell on the land because of his disobedience, Ahaz continued down the path of rebellion by hiring mercenary nations to protect him against his enemies rather than simply repenting and getting right with God. Not surprisingly, that plan failed miserably. But it is in verse nineteen that we find something that most people in our day simply skim over without even recognizing, but absolutely no one in that day would skim over without recognizing. We twice find the name Judah because that is the nation over which Ahaz was king. But right smack dab in the middle of those we find Ahaz called the "king of Israel."

But he wasn't the king of Israel. He was the king of Judah. So why would God have the writer call him that? I believe we can find the answer in verse two:

2 Chronicles 28:2 *For he walked in the ways of the kings of Israel...*

It is as if God said, "So you want to be a fanboy of wicked Israel while sitting on the throne of Judah? Fine. I will, therefore, not even allow you to be fully regarded as a king of Judah. I will tag you with the label of the inferior kingdom that is going to fall long before Judah ever does."

Ouch. DO be careful who you become a "fan" of. Often, one of God's most fitting judgments is having people labeled with the idiots they idolize!

Personal Notes:

_____

_____

_____

_____

_____

_____

_____

_____

_____

_____

_____

_____

_____

_____

_____

_____

_____

Devotion 45

God's diatribe against wicked King Ahaz of Judah (whom He insultingly labeled as king of Israel) was continuing on.

2 Chronicles 28:20 *And Tilgathpilneser king of Assyria came unto him, and distressed him, but strengthened him not.* **21** *For Ahaz took away a portion out of the house of the LORD, and out of the house of the king, and of the princes, and gave it unto the king of Assyria: but he helped him not.*

In verses twenty and twenty-one, we find Ahaz robbing the house of God and extorting his princes and even plundering the wealth of the palace and using that treasure to hire the king of Assyria to get him out of his trouble. And I know this will come as an absolute shock to you (he wrote with great sarcasm), but the thugs he hired to help him just took his money, didn't help him, and then came and robbed him.

But the worst part of it all is found in verse twenty-two, which says, *"And in the time of his distress did he trespass yet more against the LORD: this is that king Ahaz."*

For people with at least a little bit of humility and a couple of functioning brain cells, this kind of distress will lead them to humble themselves before the Lord and get right. But for anyone like Ahaz with no humility and no brain cells that seem to work properly, the obvious course is to double down on the sin and stupidity and make things worse. Ahaz did so.

And that leads us to the hilarious epithet of verse twenty-two, *"this is that King Ahaz."*

Think "Ohhhh, you mean THAT Ahaz!"

God help us when we are so stubborn and stupid that we end up as THAT Bob or Tom or Sally or Fred or Sue. DO have enough humility and intelligence not to be THAT "fill in the blank with your name."

Personal Notes:

_____

_____

_____

_____

_____

_____

_____

_____

_____

_____

_____

_____

_____

_____

_____

_____

_____

_____

_____

_____

_____

_____

Devotion 46

We now come to the last few filthy gasps of wicked king Ahaz. If consistency in wickedness no matter the result is what one was looking for, the man did not disappoint.

2 Chronicles 28:23 *For he sacrificed unto the gods of Damascus, which smote him: and he said, Because the gods of the kings of Syria help them, therefore will I sacrifice to them, that they may help me. But they were the ruin of him, and of all Israel.* **24** *And Ahaz gathered together the vessels of the house of God, and cut in pieces the vessels of the house of God, and shut up the doors of the house of the LORD, and he made him altars in every corner of Jerusalem.* **25** *And in every several city of Judah he made high places to burn incense unto other gods, and provoked to anger the LORD God of his fathers.* **26** *Now the rest of his acts and of all his ways, first and last, behold, they are written in the book of the kings of Judah and Israel.* **27** *And Ahaz slept with his fathers, and they buried him in the city, even in Jerusalem: but they brought him not into the sepulchres of the kings of Israel: and Hezekiah his son reigned in his stead.*

Not content simply with worshipping idols while others continued to worship Jehovah, Ahaz went into the very Temple of God, took the magnificent vessels that Solomon had made for worship, and cut them into pieces. Then he literally barred the door of the Temple and refused to let anyone in. Then he made altars to idols in every corner of Jerusalem and made incense altars to idols in "every several city," meaning every last one, even the tiniest.

Ahaz's philosophy seems to have been, "Worshipping these idols has not worked at all, so I need to do a bunch more of it so it finally will work!" He would have made a great modern-day socialist...

DO have enough sense to see the results of sin and to realize that those results are not going to get any better by you simply "trying harder" in that sin!

Personal Notes:

_____

_____

_____

_____

_____

_____

_____

_____

_____

_____

_____

_____

_____

_____

_____

_____

_____

_____

Devotion 47

The last words of 2 Chronicles 28 are happy, marvelous, glorious words...

2 Chronicles 28:27 *And Ahaz slept with his fathers, and they buried him in the city, even in Jerusalem: but they brought him not into the sepulchres of the kings of Israel: and Hezekiah his son reigned in his stead.*

Hezekiah. Going from Ahaz being king to Hezekiah being king would be much akin to going from Hitler being president to Billy Graham being president. And what makes it all the more remarkable is that this good and godly king was the son of ungodly Ahaz. And do you remember what one of the last filthy things was that Ahaz did? He ripped up the vessels of the Temple and barred the doors so no one could get in. But look at the first thing that his son did when he became king:

2 Chronicles 29:3 *He in the first year of his reign, in the first month, opened the doors of the house of the LORD, and repaired them.*

Daddy shut the doors. Hezekiah, his son, opened them. How wonderful! And how sad. How sad that a son had to undo the wickedness of his own father before he could even get started good in his own life. And yet that same scenario often plays itself out in our day, as children who want to live for God have to step across the wreckage that godless parents have placed in front of them to do so. The best thing any parent can spend their time in is living so godly themselves that their children, when they start their own adult lives, can rocket out of the starting gate rather than crawling across wreckage!

DO give your children the best possible advantage any parent can ever give a child; give them a high and clean platform of righteousness that they can start on as they build even higher for God!

Personal Notes:

_____

_____

_____

_____

_____

_____

_____

_____

_____

_____

_____

_____

_____

_____

_____

_____

_____

_____

_____

_____

_____

_____

_____

Devotion 48

Just opening the house of God for worship was not enough for Hezekiah. He would undo, not just the physical damage caused by his father, but the spiritual damage as well.

2 Chronicles 29:3 *He in the first year of his reign, in the first month, opened the doors of the house of the LORD, and repaired them.* **4** *And he brought in the priests and the Levites, and gathered them together into the east street,* **5** *And said unto them, Hear me, ye Levites, sanctify now yourselves, and sanctify the house of the LORD God of your fathers, and carry forth the filthiness out of the holy place.* **6** *For our fathers have trespassed, and done that which was evil in the eyes of the LORD our God, and have forsaken him, and have turned away their faces from the habitation of the LORD, and turned their backs.* **7** *Also they have shut up the doors of the porch, and put out the lamps, and have not burned incense nor offered burnt offerings in the holy place unto the God of Israel.* **8** *Wherefore the wrath of the LORD was upon Judah and Jerusalem, and he hath delivered them to trouble, to astonishment, and to hissing, as ye see with your eyes.* **9** *For, lo, our fathers have fallen by the sword, and our sons and our daughters and our wives are in captivity for this.* **10** *Now it is in mine heart to make a covenant with the LORD God of Israel, that his fierce wrath may turn away from us.* **11** *My sons, be not now negligent: for the LORD hath chosen you to stand before him, to* *serve him, and that ye should minister unto him, and burn incense.*

Hezekiah was a king, not a member of the clergy. And yet, as should actually be the case with all of us no matter our position in life, he had a deep understanding of the things of God. In these verses, he mentioned the lamps that were never supposed to go out, the burning of incense, the burnt offerings, and the fact that God had specifically appointed the Levites to stand before God and perform all of these tasks. Little wonder, then, that he was so successful in all that he did!

DO be a diligent student of the Word of God. It is not a "preacher" book; it is a "person who loves God" book!

Personal Notes:

_____

_____

_____

_____

_____

_____

_____

_____

_____

_____

_____

_____

_____

_____

_____

Devotion 49

King Hezekiah had commanded the priests to clean the house of God and get it ready for worship. And those men more than rose to the occasion.

2 Chronicles 29:16 *And the priests went into the inner part of the house of the LORD, to cleanse it, and brought out all the uncleanness that they found in the temple of the LORD into the court of the house of the LORD. And the Levites took it, to carry it out abroad into the brook Kidron.* **17** *Now they began on the first day of the first month to sanctify, and on the eighth day of the month came they to the porch of the LORD: so they sanctified the house of the LORD in eight days; and in the sixteenth day of the first month they made an end.* **18** *Then they went in to Hezekiah the king, and said, We have cleansed all the house of the LORD, and the altar of burnt offering, with all the vessels thereof, and the shewbread table, with all the vessels thereof.* **19** *Moreover all the vessels, which king Ahaz in his reign did cast away in his transgression, have we prepared and sanctified, and, behold, they are before the altar of the LORD.*

These men took sixteen total days, working like fiends, and undid the damage that King Ahaz had done over years of his wicked reign. And one part of their work was both poetic and remarkable. In 2 Chronicles 28:24, Ahaz cut the vessels of the house of God in pieces. But here in 2 Chronicles 29:19, the priests had made all of that right. Every vessel was once again whole, purified, and ready for use. It does not say they were replaced; it says they were "prepared." They were, in the words of the priests, the very vessels that Ahaz "cast away."

In other words, these men picked up the broken pieces, repaired everything, and made them ready for use. My, my, what a good picture of what God does with vessels that the devil has shattered and discarded in his wickedness!

Do you feel broken and useless? DO rejoice in knowing that there is a God in heaven who delights in rebuilding and reusing broken things!

Personal Notes:

_____

_____

_____

_____

_____

_____

_____

_____

_____

_____

_____

_____

_____

_____

_____

_____

_____

_____

Devotion 50

The Temple and the vessels were ready. All that was left now was to meet for worship.

2 Chronicles 29:20 *Then Hezekiah the king rose early, and gathered the rulers of the city, and went up to the house of the LORD.* **21** *And they brought seven bullocks, and seven rams, and seven lambs, and seven he goats, for a sin offering for the kingdom, and for the sanctuary, and for Judah. And he commanded the priests the sons of Aaron to offer them on the altar of the LORD.* **22** *So they killed the bullocks, and the priests received the blood, and sprinkled it on the altar: likewise, when they had killed the rams, they sprinkled the blood upon the altar: they killed also the lambs, and they sprinkled the blood upon the altar.* **23** *And they brought forth the he goats for the sin offering before the king and the congregation; and they laid their hands upon them:* **24** *And the priests killed them, and they made reconciliation with their blood upon the altar, to make an atonement for all Israel: for the king commanded that the burnt offering and the sin offering should be made for all Israel.* **25** *And he set the Levites in the house of the LORD with cymbals, with psalteries, and with harps, according to the commandment of David, and of Gad the king's seer, and Nathan the prophet: for so was the commandment of the LORD by his prophets.* **26** *And the Levites stood with the instruments of David, and the priests with the trumpets.* **27** *And Hezekiah commanded to offer the burnt offering upon the altar. And when the burnt* *offering began, the song of the LORD began also with the trumpets, and with the instruments ordained by David king of Israel.* **28** *And all the congregation worshipped, and the singers sang, and the trumpeters sounded: and all this continued until the burnt offering was finished.*

Offerings, singing, worship, Scripture, this was a service at the House of God. It was ungodly Ahaz who neglected it and then stopped it altogether, and it was godly Hezekiah who brought it back. It will always be the ungodly who neglect or hate meeting to worship God, and it will always be the godly who truly love it.

DO be a Hezekiah when it comes to the House of God, not an Ahaz!

Personal Notes:

_____

_____

_____

_____

_____

_____

_____

_____

_____

_____

_____

_____

_____

_____

_____

Devotion 51

The worship service was on. But it quickly grew so big that some adjustments needed to be made.

2 Chronicles 29:31 *Then Hezekiah answered and said, Now ye have consecrated yourselves unto the LORD, come near and bring sacrifices and thank offerings into the house of the LORD. And the congregation brought in sacrifices and thank offerings; and as many as were of a free heart burnt offerings.* **32** *And the number of the burnt offerings, which the congregation brought, was threescore and ten bullocks, an hundred rams, and two hundred lambs: all these were for a burnt offering to the LORD.* **33** *And the consecrated things were six hundred oxen and three thousand sheep.* **34** *But the priests were too few, so that they could not flay all the burnt offerings: wherefore their brethren the Levites did help them, till the work was ended, and until the other priests had sanctified themselves: for the Levites were more upright in heart to sanctify themselves than the priests.* **35** *And also the burnt offerings were in abundance, with the fat of the peace offerings, and the drink offerings for every burnt offering. So the service of the house of the LORD was set in order.* **36** *And Hezekiah rejoiced, and all the people, that God had prepared the people: for the thing was done suddenly.*

The offering was so big that day, the Levites had to join in with the priests to handle it. The House of God was up and running again in earnest. But the last phrase is perhaps the best part of all: *"Hezekiah rejoiced, and all the people, that God had prepared the people: for the thing was done suddenly."*

From a wrecked hull to a restored, cleaned, supplied House of God with all worship fully restored took just sixteen days. Clearly, Hezekiah had never heard of committees...

In seriousness, while such things may have their place, they can also be debilitating and utterly inefficient. Thank God for churches who keep everything accountable, and yet at the same time keep things simple enough to work quickly and get things done.

Let's always DO it that way!

Personal Notes:

_____

_____

_____

_____

_____

_____

_____

_____

_____

_____

_____

_____

_____

_____

_____

_____

_____

Devotion 52

In just sixteen days, the house of God which had been desecrated and blocked off by wicked King Ahaz was cleansed and repaired and ready for worship under godly King Hezekiah. And as the next chapter begins, something of a truly remarkable nature is noted, yet it is something that most people simply gloss over without paying much attention to.

2 Chronicles 30:1 *And Hezekiah sent to all Israel and Judah, and wrote letters also to Ephraim and Manasseh, that they should come to the house of the LORD at Jerusalem, to keep the passover unto the LORD God of Israel.*

For roughly two hundred fifty years, Israel and Judah had been two separate nations, split apart by the arrogance and stupidity of King Rehoboam. The northern kingdom of Israel never had a single godly king and, for the most part, worshipped the golden calves of Jeroboam. But here we find King Hezekiah of the southern kingdom of Judah inviting all of Israel, the northern kingdom, to come to Jerusalem to keep the Passover of the LORD. And in order to do this, he would have to have gotten permission from Hoshea, the current king of Israel. How in the world did he manage to do that?

By this time, both golden calves had already been carried away by Assyria. And so, with a vacuum in their souls, at least a few people in the northern kingdom were willing to entertain the idea of once again seeking out the one true God, the God whom they had once claimed as their own.

It is sad to realize that it often takes great loss to make people turn their thoughts toward God. But it is also encouraging to realize that no matter why people turn their thoughts toward God, He is still where He has always been and is still willing to receive the repentant in heart.

DO be encouraged; you may waver, but God never does!

Personal Notes:

_____

_____

_____

_____

_____

_____

_____

_____

_____

_____

_____

_____

_____

_____

_____

_____

_____

_____

_____

_____

_____

_____

Devotion 53

King Hezekiah was determined to have the entire nation observe the Passover as they used to do. But there was a bit of a problem with the timing.

2 Chronicles 30:2 *For the king had taken counsel, and his princes, and all the congregation in Jerusalem, to keep the passover in the second month.* **3** *For they could not keep it at that time, because the priests had not sanctified themselves sufficiently, neither had the people gathered themselves together to Jerusalem.* **4** *And the thing pleased the king and all the congregation.* **5** *So they established a decree to make proclamation throughout all Israel, from Beersheba even to Dan, that they should come to keep the passover unto the LORD God of Israel at Jerusalem: for they had not done it of a long time in such sort as it was written.*

By law, the Passover was supposed to be held on the fourteenth day of the first month. But in rare cases when a person was away on a far journey or had been accidentally defiled, that individual was allowed to observe the Passover exactly one month later. But in this case, because of the time it took to repair and cleanse the Temple, and because the entire nation was late to arrive, and because the priests and Levites had been so lackadaisical about making themselves ceremonially pure, it was literally the entire nation that was not ready! There was no provision in the law for that sort of thing. By the letter of the law, they should have waited another full year.

But Hezekiah understood something that Christ Himself often had to explain to the dull-witted, hard-nosed Pharisees of His day. While the letter of the law is important, the spirit of the law is even more so! Hezekiah knew that things could not and would not be "just right" in this worship service if they held it in the second month. But he also knew that, with just a tiny spark of revival finally taking hold in the land, a delay of a year would be like an ocean of cold water poured on that spark.

There is a lesson in that. Never let the perfect be the enemy of the good. God is more pleased with a group of worshippers who actually show up to His house and worship Him, imperfections and all, than He is with those who stay home and piously snort at things not being "decent and in order."

DO strive to be perfect in all things before God. But DO also refuse to use the quest for "perfection" as an excuse to stay home and not join in with the "good!"

Personal Notes:

_____

_____

_____

_____

_____

_____

_____

_____

_____

_____

Devotion 54

We now come to the text of the letter that King Hezekiah sent to both Israel and Judah concerning the upcoming Passover.

2 Chronicles 30:6 *So the posts went with the letters from the king and his princes throughout all Israel and Judah, and according to the commandment of the king, saying, Ye children of Israel, turn again unto the LORD God of Abraham, Isaac, and Israel, and he will return to the remnant of you, that are escaped out of the hand of the kings of Assyria. 7 And be not ye like your fathers, and like your brethren, which trespassed against the LORD God of their fathers, who therefore gave them up to desolation, as ye see. 8 Now be ye not stiffnecked, as your fathers were, but yield yourselves unto the LORD, and enter into his sanctuary, which he hath sanctified for ever: and serve the LORD your God, that the fierceness of his wrath may turn away from you. 9 For if ye turn again unto the LORD, your brethren and your children shall find compassion before them that lead them captive, so that they shall come again into this land: for the LORD your God is gracious and merciful, and will not turn away his face from you, if ye return unto him.*

There are three key words that Hezekiah gave the two kingdoms one after the other, the words turn, yield, and serve. Those words perfectly describe what must happen in the heart of a backslidden nation or even just a backslidden person if they are to ever truly be right with God. And if a person will "turn" from their sin, "yield" to the will of God for their life, and truly "serve" God with all their heart, they will find the conclusion of Hezekiah's words in verse nine to be true: *"the LORD your God is gracious and merciful, and will not turn away his face from you, if ye return unto him."*

If you are not where you are supposed to be with God, DO turn, yield, and serve!

Personal Notes:

_____

_____

_____

_____

_____

_____

_____

_____

_____

_____

_____

_____

_____

_____

_____

_____

_____

_____

_____

_____

_____

_____

Devotion 55

Hezekiah's letter had gone out to both kingdoms. Now the only question was, how would it be received? Here is the answer to that question.

2 Chronicles 30:10 *So the posts passed from city to city through the country of Ephraim and Manasseh even unto Zebulun: but they laughed them to scorn, and mocked them.*

The first group of people we see in this passage not only declined to come to the re-instituted Passover, they actually laughed and mocked the messengers inviting them to come. They thought it was the biggest joke in the world.

But others felt differently.

2 Chronicles 30:11 *Nevertheless divers* [many] *of Asher and Manasseh and of Zebulun humbled themselves, and came to Jerusalem.* **12** *Also in Judah the hand of God was to give them one heart to do the commandment of the king and of the princes, by the word of the LORD.* **13** *And there assembled at Jerusalem much people to keep the feast of unleavened bread in the second month, a very great congregation.*

Everyone had a free will. Some used it to harden their hearts and mock and jeer. Others used it to humble their hearts and come to God's house and worship. And while the mockers doubtless enjoyed their mocking, they missed what became the second most famous Passover celebration in the history of the nation up to that time.

Everyone still has a free will and the same choices to make. DO choose to be among the worshippers, not the mockers!

Personal Notes:

_____

_____

_____

_____

_____

_____

_____

_____

_____

_____

_____

_____

_____

_____

_____

_____

_____

_____

_____

_____

_____

_____

_____

_____

_____

Devotion 56

The worship service was on in earnest. And it had results way before "the invitation" and way beyond just the people in "the pews."

2 Chronicles 30:14 *And they arose and took away the altars that were in Jerusalem, and all the altars for incense took they away, and cast them into the brook Kidron.* **15** *Then they killed the passover on the fourteenth day of the second month: and the priests and the Levites were ashamed, and sanctified themselves, and brought in the burnt offerings into the house of the LORD.*

In verse fourteen we find they, meaning the people, physically picked up all of the altars and items of heathenism and chucked them into the river. Then they prepared the Passover lamb and meal and festivities. And it is then that we find that *"the Levites were ashamed, and sanctified themselves, and brought in the burnt offerings into the house of the LORD."* In other words, the "clergy" was sitting back doing nothing, expecting all of the religious fervor to simply die down. But when it did not, they got embarrassed by how on fire for God the people were, and they decided to join them!

That seems a bit backwards, doesn't it? And yet there is nothing in Scripture that indicates that all "fervor" needs to come from the pulpit. In fact, it would do many churches good to have the people get so on fire for God that the pastor rushes to catch up with them rather than having the pastor constantly trying to start a fire with only wet logs to work with!

DO get so on fire for God that everyone else is left scrambling to catch up and join in!

Personal Notes:

_____
_____
_____
_____
_____
_____
_____
_____
_____
_____
_____
_____
_____
_____
_____
_____
_____
_____
_____
_____
_____
_____
_____
_____
_____
_____
_____

Devotion 57

The worship service was still going on hot. And yet, just as with the timing of the service, the people themselves were also not "perfect" according to the letter of the law for all of this.

2 Chronicles 30:16 *And they stood in their place after their manner, according to the law of Moses the man of God: the priests sprinkled the blood, which they received of the hand of the Levites.* **17** *For there were many in the congregation that were not sanctified: therefore the Levites had the charge of the killing of the passovers for every one that was not clean, to sanctify them unto the LORD.* **18** *For a multitude of the people, even many of Ephraim, and Manasseh, Issachar, and Zebulun, had not cleansed themselves, yet did they eat the passover otherwise than it was written. But Hezekiah prayed for them, saying, The good LORD pardon every one* **19** *That prepareth his heart to seek God, the LORD God of his fathers, though he be not cleansed according to the purification of the sanctuary.*

By the letter of the law, there was an elaborate system of ritual purification that every person was to undergo before worshipping at the Passover. But since it had been generations since the Passover had even been held, people did not even know any of this anymore, and thus came up to the Passover ceremonially unclean. By the letter of the law, they should have been barred from worship. But Hezekiah got it right yet again, saying, *"The good LORD pardon every one that prepareth his heart to seek*

God, the LORD God of his fathers, though he be not cleansed according to the purification of the sanctuary."

There would be time for getting the letter of the law right as people grew in the Lord and renewed their study of Scripture. But for now, just getting them to the Passover with hearts prepared to seek the LORD was what mattered most.

We often put the cart before the horse on this. People who are untrained in the ways of the Lord should not be expected to look and act like veteran believers before being allowed to come and worship. DO extend boatloads of grace and patience to people who have as far to go now as you did way back when you were a new believer!

Personal Notes:

_____
_____
_____
_____
_____
_____
_____
_____
_____
_____
_____
_____
_____
_____
_____

Devotion 58

This amazing Passover service, followed by the feast of unleavened bread, would have been utterly unthinkable just a short time before under King Ahaz. But his son, King Hezekiah, so understood the heart of God that he made it all happen. And rather than being a rigid, cold observance, it was full of grace and life. And that caused the most amazing thing to happen:

2 Chronicles 30:21 *And the children of Israel that were present at Jerusalem kept the feast of unleavened bread seven days with great gladness: and the Levites and the priests praised the LORD day by day, singing with loud instruments unto the LORD.* **22** *And Hezekiah spake comfortably unto all the Levites that taught the good knowledge of the LORD: and they did eat throughout the feast seven days, offering peace offerings, and making confession to the LORD God of their fathers.* **23** *And the whole assembly took counsel to keep other seven days: and they kept other seven days with gladness.*

The "revival," if you will, was scheduled to run seven days. But God so moved in everyone's heart that they ran it an additional seven days! These people were hungry for God and for the Word of God and were happy to be at His house worshipping with everyone else.

What people give their time to is a great indicator of what they actually hunger for, and what they hunger for is a great indicator of the condition of their heart. No one in the days of Ahaz cared about going to the house of God and worshipping. But under King Hezekiah they all got right with God and could not get enough of it. Oh that people would hunger so today!

DO evaluate what you truly hunger for!

Personal Notes:

_____

_____

_____

_____

_____

_____

_____

_____

_____

_____

_____

_____

_____

_____

_____

_____

_____

_____

_____

_____

_____

_____

_____

_____

_____

Devotion 59

The epic Passover feast plus the fourteen-day worship service that followed was finally done. Now the only question that remained was, "Was this is just some emotional service, or was there actually something real about it?"

How often have we seen or heard of "out of the banks services" or "multi-week, heaven sent revivals" that somehow left people and a church and an area in the exact same condition as they were before all of that?

The very first verse of the next chapter answers that question for us.

2 Chronicles 31:1 *Now when all this was finished, all Israel that were present went out to the cities of Judah, and brake the images in pieces, and cut down the groves, and threw down the high places and the altars out of all Judah and Benjamin, in Ephraim also and Manasseh, until they had utterly destroyed them all. Then all the children of Israel returned, every man to his possession, into their own cities.*

When the revival was done, everyone went out and destroyed all of their idols. This was not just an emotional moment during worship; it was a very real change that was evidenced by a return to holiness in everyday living. Lots of people claim to be walking close to God... and to love Him more than anything... and to be so happy in Jesus... and yet they still live like the devil. There is not a single reason to actually believe that such a "walk with God" is actually real!

Throughout Scripture when people were truly right with God, they consistently cleaned the sin out of their lives and lived holy.

God is not impressed by cute social media posts supposedly praising Him. He is impressed by people whose holy lives actually prove that they love Him and live for Him. So DO be real; DO be holy!

Personal Notes:

_____

_____

_____

_____

_____

_____

_____

_____

_____

_____

_____

_____

_____

_____

_____

_____

_____

_____

_____

_____

_____

_____

_____

Devotion 60

The revival was done, everyone went out and burned and destroyed their idols, and now all that was left was to make sure that the house of God continued to be strong for the long term. And, since Hezekiah knew the Scripture, he knew just how to make that happen as well.

2 Chronicles 31:5 *And as soon as the commandment came abroad, the children of Israel brought in abundance the firstfruits of corn, wine, and oil, and honey, and of all the increase of the field; and the tithe of all things brought they in abundantly.* **6** *And concerning the children of Israel and Judah, that dwelt in the cities of Judah, they also brought in the tithe of oxen and sheep, and the tithe of holy things which were consecrated unto the LORD their God, and laid them by heaps.* **7** *In the third month they began to lay the foundation of the heaps, and finished them in the seventh month.* **8** *And when Hezekiah and the princes came and saw the heaps, they blessed the LORD, and his people Israel.* **9** *Then Hezekiah questioned with the priests and the Levites concerning the heaps.* **10** *And Azariah the chief priest of the house of Zadok answered him, and said, Since the people began to bring the offerings into the house of the LORD, we have had enough to eat, and have left plenty: for the LORD hath blessed his people; and that which is left is this great store.* **11** *Then Hezekiah commanded to prepare chambers in the house of the LORD; and they prepared them,* **12** *And brought in the offerings and the tithes and the dedicated things* *faithfully: over which Cononiah the Levite was ruler, and Shimei his brother was the next.*

At the commandment of the king, who was simply repeating the command of God in Scripture, everyone started tithing, and even giving offering over and above their tithes. The house of God instantly had a great surplus that would keep the work going strong for a very long time.

When people have truly gotten right with God, this will never be an issue. Wicked people in the days of wicked Ahaz did not tithe, godly people in the days of godly Hezekiah did!

DO be among the latter rather than the former!

Personal Notes:

_____

_____

_____

_____

_____

_____

_____

_____

_____

_____

_____

_____

_____

_____

_____

_____

_____

Devotion 61

Hezekiah was so very successful after his father had been such a failure. What was his secret?

2 Chronicles 31:20 *And thus did Hezekiah throughout all Judah, and wrought that which was good and right and truth before the LORD his God.* **21** *And in every work that he began in the service of the house of God, and in the law, and in the commandments, to seek his God, he did it with all his heart, and prospered.*

Hezekiah wrought, worked at, that which was good and right and true before the LORD. And in reference to what he did in the house of God, and in the law, and in the commandments, it was all to seek after God, and he did it all with all of his heart.

As I put it so often, "All out, all for God, all the time!"

People who "just sort of follow God" almost inevitably stop following altogether, just as sheep who lag far behind the shepherd almost always eventually wander off into the wilderness and get lost then devoured. Being successful in our walk with God is largely a matter of proximity and passion; we are supposed to walk very close to God, and we are to do so while putting all of our heart into that walk with God!

DO go all out, all for God, all the time!

Personal Notes:

Devotion 62

Sometimes big truths hang on small words. And that is certainly the case as we enter a new chapter describing the reign of godly King Hezekiah.

2 Chronicles 32:1 *After these things, and the establishment thereof, Sennacherib king of Assyria came, and entered into Judah, and encamped against the fenced cities, and thought to win them for himself.*

It would seem like the huge and important words in this verse would be words like Sennacherib, king of Assyria, entered into Judah, encamped against, and thought to win them for himself.

But the three seemingly innocuous words that started this verse, *"after these things,"* are just as important or more so than all of those other words. The "things" that this invasion came after were the removal of all of the idolatrous images and altars from the land, the renovation and sanctification of the Temple, and the re-establishment of the pure worship of Jehovah God among the people. In fact, the timeline of this event in 2 Kings lets us know that this was actually fourteen years after those things! God was so pleased by what He was seeing that He kept the devil at bay for fourteen years until everyone could get good and settled in to truly following the Lord again.

There is no doubt whatsoever that the devil would love to have attacked immediately, while they were weak. But in this instance, God did not let it happen.

The devil is not just on a leash, he is also on a schedule! God not only reigns him in, He also regulates his timetable for him.

DO worship God so passionately that when the devil comes asking Him for permission to torment you, He says, "Not yet; I am busy enjoying the worship!"

Personal Notes:

_____

_____

_____

_____

_____

_____

_____

_____

_____

_____

_____

_____

_____

_____

_____

_____

_____

_____

_____

_____

Devotion 63

Hezekiah, the king, knew that the Assyrians were invading the land and coming for Jerusalem. And while he prayed, he also prepared, and that is a great pattern for us to follow.

2 Chronicles 32:2 *And when Hezekiah saw that Sennacherib was come, and that he was purposed to fight against Jerusalem,* **3** *He took counsel with his princes and his mighty men to stop the waters of the fountains which were without the city: and they did help him.* **4** *So there was gathered much people together, who stopped all the fountains, and the brook that ran through the midst of the land, saying, Why should the kings of Assyria come, and find much water?*

There is so much wisdom in what they did. Since they knew the fountainheads and the Assyrians did not, they simply stopped them all up, knowing they could fix it later if they survived. Their reasoning was that it was foolish to allow the enemy to drink your own water while attacking you. In other words, they were not going to help the enemy destroy them.

But many times, that is exactly what we do. We live lives that allow our enemy (the devil and those who serve him) to destroy us. They do not even have to "bring their own water," they just use ours. DO be wise enough to live such a pure and godly life that if the devil wants to come against you and destroy you, he has to carry his own water to do it!

Personal Notes:

_____
_____
_____
_____
_____
_____
_____
_____
_____
_____
_____
_____
_____
_____
_____
_____
_____
_____
_____
_____
_____
_____
_____
_____
_____
_____
_____
_____

Devotion 64

Hezekiah and his men, knowing that Sennacherib and Assyria were heading that way, had stopped up the fountains of water so that the Assyrians would not be able to easily get water to drink while they besieged them. Here is what the text tells us came next:

2 Chronicles 32:5 *Also he strengthened himself, and built up all the wall that was broken, and raised it up to the towers, and another wall without, and repaired Millo in the city of David, and made darts and shields in abundance.* **6** *And he set captains of war over the people, and gathered them together to him in the street of the gate of the city, and spake comfortably to them, saying,* **7** *Be strong and courageous, be not afraid nor dismayed for the king of Assyria, nor for all the multitude that is with him: for there be more with us than with him:* **8** *With him is an arm of flesh; but with us is the LORD our God to help us, and to fight our battles. And the people rested themselves upon the words of Hezekiah king of Judah.*

The most obvious thing to behold in this passage is the building of walls and towers and weapons. But, as important as those things were, those things were not what gave the frightened people the confidence to persevere. Verse six tells us that the king spoke comforting words to them, specifically words of how great God is, and the people rested themselves on his words, not on weapons or walls.

People are often hurting, uncertain, and even scared. And the words we speak can easily be the very thing they need to make it through another day.

DO find someone to encourage today, someone to reconcile with today, someone to point toward God today, someone to cheer today!

Personal Notes:

_____

_____

_____

_____

_____

_____

_____

_____

_____

_____

_____

_____

_____

_____

_____

_____

_____

_____

_____

_____

_____

_____

Devotion 65

Battles in the ancient world were almost always religious battles as much as political battles, and this one was no exception. And that is why we find Sennacherib, king of Assyria, "waxing theological" in a message he sent to the besieged city of Jerusalem. The only problem was his "theology" was just about as off base as most of the internet theologians of our own day.

2 Chronicles 32:9 *After this did Sennacherib king of Assyria send his servants to Jerusalem, (but he himself laid siege against Lachish, and all his power with him,) unto Hezekiah king of Judah, and unto all Judah that were at Jerusalem, saying,* **10** *Thus saith Sennacherib king of Assyria, Whereon do ye trust, that ye abide in the siege in Jerusalem?* **11** *Doth not Hezekiah persuade you to give over yourselves to die by famine and by thirst, saying, The LORD our God shall deliver us out of the hand of the king of Assyria?* **12** *Hath not the same Hezekiah taken away his high places and his altars, and commanded Judah and Jerusalem, saying, Ye shall worship before one altar, and burn incense upon it?*

When the elders of Judah read this, their reaction must have been, "Uh, wait, what?"

In case you do not know, the high places and altars that Hezekiah removed were pagan altars to pagan idols erected by his pagan father, Ahaz.

There is a lesson in that. Not everyone who sounds like a theologian actually is. So DO be careful whose post you like, share, or promote!

Personal Notes:

_____
_____
_____
_____
_____
_____
_____
_____
_____
_____
_____
_____
_____
_____
_____
_____
_____
_____
_____
_____
_____
_____
_____
_____
_____
_____
_____
_____

Devotion 66

As Sennacherib's servants continued to shout at the Jews on the walls of Jerusalem, giving them the message of Sennacherib, the subject continued to be "theology."

2 Chronicles 32:13 *Know ye not what I and my fathers have done unto all the people of other lands? were the gods of the nations of those lands any ways able to deliver their lands out of mine hand?* **14** *Who was there among all the gods of those nations that my fathers utterly destroyed, that could deliver his people out of mine hand, that your God should be able to deliver you out of mine hand?* **15** *Now therefore let not Hezekiah deceive you, nor persuade you on this manner, neither yet believe him: for no god of any nation or kingdom was able to deliver his people out of mine hand, and out of the hand of my fathers: how much less shall your God deliver you out of mine hand?* **16** *And his servants spake yet more against the LORD God, and against his servant Hezekiah.* **17** *He wrote also letters to rail on the LORD God of Israel, and to speak against him, saying, As the gods of the nations of other lands have not delivered their people out of mine hand, so shall not the God of Hezekiah deliver his people out of mine hand.*

Those words are pretty repetitive, don't you think? Four times he pointed out that the gods of other nations had not delivered them from Assyria, and that therefore God would not deliver the Jews. To Sennacherib, the proof of god/God was in the endurance or fall of his/His people. He would soon regret those words as God, the real God, did in fact deliver His people from this mouthy monarch.

But in the words of Ron Popeil, "But wait, there's more!"

If you go to the Middle East today, in the 21st century, Israel is still there in that exact same spot, still surviving and thriving. But in 612 B.C., Assyria fell to the Babylonians, and even its ruins were covered by sand and un-viewed by human eyes for more than 2,000 years. The fact that Israel survived Assyria and Babylon and Greece and Rome and 2,000 years of exile and Adolf Hitler himself is clear proof that their God, our God, is alive and real!

DO be confident in your God; history is HISstory!

Personal Notes:

_____
_____
_____
_____
_____
_____
_____
_____
_____
_____
_____
_____
_____

Devotion 67

The Assyrian army outside the gates was no idle threat. Everyone knew that they could very well be wiped off the face of the earth. And thus we find prophet and King, "church and state," if you will, coming together for a prayer meeting.

2 Chronicles 32:18 *Then they cried with a loud voice in the Jews' speech unto the people of Jerusalem that were on the wall, to affright them, and to trouble them; that they might take the city.* **19** *And they spake against the God of Jerusalem, as against the gods of the people of the earth, which were the work of the hands of man.* **20** *And for this cause Hezekiah the king, and the prophet Isaiah the son of Amoz, prayed and cried to heaven.*

Isaiah and Hezekiah. The preacher and the politician. And what was the result of *gasp* "bringing God into political issues?"

2 Chronicles 32:21 *And the LORD sent an angel, which cut off all the mighty men of valour, and the leaders and captains in the camp of the king of Assyria. So he returned with shame of face to his own land. And when he was come into the house of his god, they that came forth of his own bowels slew him there with the sword.* **22** *Thus the LORD saved Hezekiah and the inhabitants of Jerusalem from the hand of Sennacherib the king of Assyria, and from the hand of all other, and guided them on every side.*

A nation with praying politicians, men and women who actually know and revere God, not just narcissists looking for a photo op, will be a blessed nation.

DO refuse to fall for the notion that the spiritual and the secular must be kept far apart in our land. We would be far better off having a revival meeting in the United States Capitol than the foolishness and filth we currently endure from Washington on a daily basis!

Personal Notes:

_____

_____

_____

_____

_____

_____

_____

_____

_____

_____

_____

_____

_____

_____

_____

_____

_____

_____

_____

_____

_____

_____

Devotion 68

After giving us the account of Jerusalem's delivery from the hands of Assyria, the text turns to a brief summary of the most miraculous episode in the life of Hezekiah—and of the foolish mistake that came after it.

2 Chronicles 32:24 *In those days Hezekiah was sick to the death, and prayed unto the LORD: and he spake unto him, and he gave him a sign.* **25** *But Hezekiah rendered not again according to the benefit done unto him; for his heart was lifted up: therefore there was wrath upon him, and upon Judah and Jerusalem.* **26** *Notwithstanding Hezekiah humbled himself for the pride of his heart, both he and the inhabitants of Jerusalem, so that the wrath of the LORD came not upon them in the days of Hezekiah.*

The fuller account of this episode is found in 2 Kings 20 and Isaiah 38. Hezekiah was told that he was going to die. He wept and begged God for mercy, and God granted him the miraculous sign of the shadow of the sundial going backward ten degrees and of fifteen more years of life.

Shortly thereafter, emissaries came calling from Babylon. In pride, Hezekiah showed them all the treasures of his house. Little wonder, then, that when Babylon got strong a few generations later, they came and destroyed Jerusalem and took all of those treasures. Yes, Hezekiah humbled himself and experienced peace in his day, but his grandchildren and great-grandchildren paid the price for his foolishness.

It is easy to move from a great victory to a great failure when we allow pride into our lives. DO think enough of your children and grandchildren to walk humbly before God!

Personal Notes:

_____

_____

_____

_____

_____

_____

_____

_____

_____

_____

_____

_____

_____

_____

_____

_____

_____

_____

_____

_____

_____

_____

_____

_____

Devotion 69

As the text begins to wrap up the life of Hezekiah, it says something that is more significant than you may imagine.

2 Chronicles 32:30 *This same Hezekiah also stopped the upper watercourse of Gihon, and brought it straight down to the west side of the city of David. And Hezekiah prospered in all his works.*

This is the biblical description of an aqueduct built by Hezekiah. But what are we often told about Scripture by scoffers? "It's just a book of fairytales!" But is that the case? Let's check in with National Geographic...

"The latest—and most impressive—of ancient Jerusalem's waterworks is probably the so-called Hezekiah's Tunnel. The construction of the subterranean feature is described in the book of Chronicles in the Bible: [Hezekiah] blocked up the upper spring of Gihon and brought the water down through a tunnel to the west side of the City of David.

"Hezekiah's Tunnel was built by King Hezekiah before 701 BCE, when it helped Jerusalem to survive the siege by King Sennacherib of Assyria," Rubin says. "It is a tunnel cut in the rock beneath the City of David leading water from the Gihon to the Siloam Pool [a freshwater reservoir fed by the tunnel]."

This amazing aqueduct is still in existence to this very day, 2,700 years later. Hooray for Hezekiah, and hooray for the Bible, a true book of history, not, as the unintelligent scoffers say, a book of fairy tales.

DO know that you can trust your Bible!

Personal Notes:

_____

_____

_____

_____

_____

_____

_____

_____

_____

_____

_____

_____

_____

_____

_____

_____

_____

_____

_____

_____

_____

_____

_____

_____

_____

Devotion 70

Let's look at the last verse of chapter thirty-two and the first two verses of chapter thirty-three as we see the ending days of Hezekiah and the beginning days of the reign of his son, Manasseh.

2 Chronicles 32:33 *And Hezekiah slept with his fathers, and they buried him in the chiefest of the sepulchres of the sons of David: and all Judah and the inhabitants of Jerusalem did him honour at his death. And Manasseh his son reigned in his stead.*

2 Chronicles 33:1 *Manasseh was twelve years old when he began to reign, and he reigned fifty and five years in Jerusalem:* **2** *But did that which was evil in the sight of the LORD, like unto the abominations of the heathen, whom the LORD had cast out before the children of Israel.*

Do you remember the account of Hezekiah being sick unto death, and what God did for him? Hezekiah was granted fifteen more years of life. And here we find that during those extra fifteen years Hezekiah finally had a son, Manasseh. Manasseh reigned for fifty-five years and was one of the most evil men who ever lived and one of the very worst monarchs to ever reign. And while our initial impression might be to regret the extra fifteen years of Hezekiah, those extra fifteen years produced the son that would continue the bloodline of the Lord Jesus Christ!

People in those days doubtless thought God had made a mistake by granting Hezekiah those extra years because of this heinous, demonic child of his.

But they only saw the immediate picture; the God who never misses anything saw things much farther down the line and acted accordingly.

Don't be too quick to see the here and now and make evaluations based on such a small snapshot; DO remember that God sees the entire picture!

Personal Notes:

_____

_____

_____

_____

_____

_____

_____

_____

_____

_____

_____

_____

_____

_____

_____

_____

_____

_____

_____

_____

_____

_____

_____

Devotion 71

With some evil kings, God just issued a summary of their wickedness. But with Manasseh, who ruled like the devil in the flesh for most of fifty-five years, God gave us a detailed list of his wickedness.

2 Chronicles 33:3 *For he built again the high places which Hezekiah his father had broken down, and he reared up altars for Baalim, and made groves, and worshipped all the host of heaven, and served them.* **4** *Also he built altars in the house of the LORD, whereof the LORD had said, In Jerusalem shall my name be for ever.* **5** *And he built altars for all the host of heaven in the two courts of the house of the LORD.* **6** *And he caused his children to pass through the fire in the valley of the son of Hinnom: also he observed times, and used enchantments, and used witchcraft, and dealt with a familiar spirit, and with wizards: he wrought much evil in the sight of the LORD, to provoke him to anger.* **7** *And he set a carved image, the idol which he had made, in the house of God, of which God had said to David and to Solomon his son, In this house, and in Jerusalem, which I have chosen before all the tribes of Israel, will I put my name for ever:*

While this list is long and damning, I am struck by how acceptable certain of the things on it are today in the eyes of man. Manasseh killed his own children, just like American society, which has slaughtered sixty-three million babies and counting worshipping at the altar of Planned Parenthood. He also "observed times," meaning that he engaged in astrology—the utilization of horoscopes. That one especially gets shrugged off today. Further, we find that he was engaged in witchcraft and wizardry. This as well has become completely palatable in our world when God called it an abomination. He also "dealt with a familiar spirit," meaning that he had communication with a demon. Even this is becoming acceptable in the modern world. One of the most famous pop stars of our day openly brags about performing under the influence of a demon.

But God's evaluation of it now is the exact same as it was in the days of Manasseh; in verse nine He said it was doing *"worse than the heathen."*

When you try today to determine whether something is right or wrong, DO look at God's Word instead of a calendar; time never changes God's evaluation of wickedness and righteousness!

Personal Notes:

_____

_____

_____

_____

_____

_____

_____

_____

_____

_____

_____

Devotion 72

Manasseh was so horribly wicked, and he dragged the entire nation into that wickedness. So, how would the all-powerful God respond?

2 Chronicles 33:10 *And the LORD spake to Manasseh, and to his people: but they would not hearken.*

He spoke to them. The God who could have immediately destroyed all of them instead simply spoke to them, telling them they were wrong and needed to change course. And yet, verse ten very clearly says that they would not listen. This is yet another example among tens of thousands in Scripture of how very foolish Calvinism is. God does not predestine our course and our decisions. We chart our own course and make our own decisions and therefore bear the responsibility for every single choice we make. And in this case, the ramifications of their decision were going to be ruinous:

2 Chronicles 33:11 *Wherefore the LORD brought upon them the captains of the host of the king of Assyria, which took Manasseh among the thorns, and bound him with fetters, and carried him to Babylon.*

Manasseh tried to hide in the thorns and brambles. It did not work. The enemies that God sent against him found him, dragged him out like some trapped animal, chained him up, and carried him away to Babylon. He learned the hard way that all of us get to choose our own path, but none of us get to choose our own consequences!

If you want all of the right results, DO make all of the right choices!

Personal Notes:

_____

_____

_____

_____

_____

_____

_____

_____

_____

_____

Devotion 73

Manasseh had reigned for twenty-two wicked years when he was turned over to his enemies by God. But that is not the end of his story. In fact, it is the end of his story that is the most interesting of all, because it is literally a one-of-a-kind story among all the kings of Israel and Judah.

2 Chronicles 33:12 *And when he was in affliction, he besought the LORD his God, and humbled himself greatly before the God of his fathers,* **13** *And prayed unto him: and he was intreated of him, and heard his supplication, and brought him again to Jerusalem into his kingdom. Then Manasseh knew that the LORD he was God.* **14** *Now after this he built a wall without the city of David, on the west side of Gihon, in the valley, even to the entering in at the fish gate, and compassed about Ophel, and raised it up a very great height, and put captains of war in all the fenced cities of Judah.* **15** *And he took away the strange gods, and the idol out of the house of the LORD, and all the altars that he had built in the mount of the house of the LORD, and in Jerusalem, and cast them out of the city.* **16** *And he repaired the altar of the LORD, and sacrificed thereon peace offerings and thank offerings, and commanded Judah to serve the LORD God of Israel.*

Not one other king in history ever lived for the devil, got taken into captivity, repented with all of his heart, was released from captivity, was put back on his throne, and went on to serve God with all of his heart for the rest of his life! Manasseh was truly amazing in this, as was the merciful God who so pardoned him.

DO remember that God's purpose in chastisement is restoration, not ruin. So DO repent of any sin and allow God to restore you while there is time!

Personal Notes:

_____

_____

_____

_____

_____

_____

_____

_____

_____

_____

_____

_____

_____

_____

_____

_____

_____

_____

_____

_____

_____

_____

_____

Devotion 74

All good things and all good kings must come to an end, and Manasseh did, leaving the throne to his son.

2 Chronicles 33:20 *So Manasseh slept with his fathers, and they buried him in his own house: and Amon his son reigned in his stead.* **21** *Amon was two and twenty years old when he began to reign, and reigned two years in Jerusalem.*

Each king that reigned had either a good example to follow when it came to their father, the previous king, or a bad example to follow. Amon actually had both! His father set an example of evil for the first twenty-two years, and then when finally released spent the last years doing right. So which "dad" would Amon emulate?

2 Chronicles 33:22 *But he did that which was evil in the sight of the LORD, as did Manasseh his father: for Amon sacrificed unto all the carved images which Manasseh his father had made, and served them;* **23** *And humbled not himself before the LORD, as Manasseh his father had humbled himself; but Amon trespassed more and more.*

Faced with a choice of which example to follow, Amon chose to follow the wrong example his father had set. And in this, he was like a lot of people today who could either follow the good of their parents or the bad and choose to indulge their flesh by following the bad.

No parent will ever be perfect since no person will ever be perfect. Since that is always the case, DO intentionally find the good in the examples of those who have come before you and follow that rather than gleefully finding the bad to follow!

Personal Notes:

_____

_____

_____

_____

_____

_____

_____

_____

_____

_____

_____

_____

_____

_____

_____

_____

_____

_____

_____

_____

_____

_____

_____

_____

_____

_____

_____

Devotion 75

Amon chose to lead wickedly after his father had repented of wickedness. And by this point in the history of the kingdom, some of the servants were not in much of a mood to be patient with a monarch who was clearly going to get them in trouble again:

2 Chronicles 33:24 *And his servants conspired against him, and slew him in his own house.* **25** *But the people of the land slew all them that had conspired against king Amon; and the people of the land made Josiah his son king in his stead.*

Manasseh ruled wickedly then repented and ruled righteously. Amon, his son, just ruled wickedly. Josiah went a different direction than either of them...

2 Chronicles 34:1 *Josiah was eight years old when he began to reign, and he reigned in Jerusalem one and thirty years.* **2** *And he did that which was right in the sight of the LORD, and walked in the ways of David his father, and declined neither to the right hand, nor to the left.*

Adam Clarke said of this amazing young king, "He never swerved from God and truth; he never omitted what he knew to be his duty to God and his kingdom; he carried on his reformation with a steady hand; timidity did not prevent him from going far enough; and zeal did not lead him beyond due bounds. He walked in the golden mean, and his moderation was known unto all men. He went neither to the right nor to the left, he looked inward, looked forward, and looked upward. Reader, let the conduct of this pious youth be thy exemplar through life."

DO follow this amazing example!

Personal Notes:

_____

_____

_____

_____

_____

_____

_____

_____

_____

_____

_____

_____

_____

_____

_____

_____

_____

_____

_____

_____

_____

_____

_____

_____

_____

_____

_____

_____

Devotion 76

As we begin to look at the life and reign of godly King Josiah, an interesting timeline is presented to us.

2 Chronicles 34:1 *Josiah was eight years old when he began to reign, and he reigned in Jerusalem one and thirty years.* **2** *And he did that which was right in the sight of the LORD, and walked in the ways of David his father, and declined neither to the right hand, nor to the left.* **3** *For in the eighth year of his reign, while he was yet young, he began to seek after the God of David his father: and in the twelfth year he began to purge Judah and Jerusalem from the high places, and the groves, and the carved images, and the molten images.*

You have perhaps already done the math in your head. But here are the details that go with that math. Josiah became king as an eight-year-old little boy. Nothing positive or negative is said at that point; he seems to have been just a good kid learning the ropes. At sixteen years of age, he began to personally seek after God. At twenty years of age, he began to actively push for righteousness all around him.

And this is very much the wonderful progression that we often see in church kids. They grow up around the things of the Lord, finally receive Him as their personal savior, and then after a few years of walking with Him personally actively begin being a force for righteousness.

Parents, DO keep your children in and around the things of the Lord early, often, and always. And kids, DO grow in the Lord every day and become a force for righteousness!

Personal Notes:

_____

_____

_____

_____

_____

_____

_____

_____

_____

_____

_____

_____

_____

_____

_____

_____

_____

_____

_____

_____

_____

_____

_____

_____

_____

_____

_____

_____

_____

Devotion 77

Once Josiah got started on his reformation for the land, he pursued it with a holy fervor.

2 Chronicles 34:4 *And they brake down the altars of Baalim in his presence; and the images, that were on high above them, he cut down; and the groves, and the carved images, and the molten images, he brake in pieces, and made dust of them, and strowed it upon the graves of them that had sacrificed unto them.* **5** *And he burnt the bones of the priests upon their altars, and cleansed Judah and Jerusalem.* **6** *And so did he in the cities of Manasseh, and Ephraim, and Simeon, even unto Naphtali, with their mattocks round about.* **7** *And when he had broken down the altars and the groves, and had beaten the graven images into powder, and cut down all the idols throughout all the land of Israel, he returned to Jerusalem.*

There are two things that I find fascinating in these verses. Number one, he made sure the altars of Baalim, were torn down "in his presence." In other words, he made sure to watch it happen with his own eyes just so that nothing would be missed. Number two, he took his godly destruction even into the territories of Manasseh, Ephraim, Simeon, and Naphtali. Those areas were the dominion of Israel, not Judah! In so many words, Josiah hauled out his trash and the neighbor's trash as well.

This is not a "casually religious guy" that you are looking at in this passage; this is a person who knows God and is serious about living for Him and serving Him. Anyone who claims to be "spiritual" and yet has no abhorrence of sin in their life or the lives of others may be "spiritual," but they are not godly.

DO be godly!

Personal Notes:

_____

_____

_____

_____

_____

_____

_____

_____

_____

_____

_____

_____

_____

_____

_____

_____

_____

_____

_____

_____

_____

_____

_____

Devotion 78

As the account of godly King Josiah continues, we next find him turning his attention to repairing and re-beautifying the house of God.

2 Chronicles 34:8 *Now in the eighteenth year of his reign, when he had purged the land, and the house, he sent Shaphan the son of Azaliah, and Maaseiah the governor of the city, and Joah the son of Joahaz the recorder, to repair the house of the LORD his God. 9 And when they came to Hilkiah the high priest, they delivered the money that was brought into the house of God, which the Levites that kept the doors had gathered of the hand of Manasseh and Ephraim, and of all the remnant of Israel, and of all Judah and Benjamin; and they returned to Jerusalem. 10 And they put it in the hand of the workmen that had the oversight of the house of the LORD, and they gave it to the workmen that wrought in the house of the LORD, to repair and amend the house: 11 Even to the artificers and builders gave they it, to buy hewn stone, and timber for couplings, and to floor the houses which the kings of Judah had destroyed.*

In verse ten, we find a general category of men who were entrusted with money and resources to fix the Temple; they were called workmen. But in verse eleven, we find two specific categories of workmen engaged in fixing the Temple, artificers and builders. Builders means exactly what you would assume it to mean: framers, construction workers. Artificers, though, means artisans. These people were engravers and other craftsmen.

It is instructive that God pointed out both of these two very different kinds of workmen for us. To put it in modern terms, you would not want your concrete men building your cabinets, nor would you want your cabinetmakers roofing your building or your framers painting your walls.

All of us have different sets of skills. But when we all put what we have to use for the Lord, a beautiful product comes from it. So DON'T despise the gifts of others, and DO use your own gifts for the Lord along with those others!

Personal Notes:

_____

_____

_____

_____

_____

_____

_____

_____

_____

_____

_____

_____

_____

_____

_____

_____

_____

_____

Devotion 79

As the account of the reparations and re-beautification of the Temple continued, we come to one of the most remarkable and heartbreaking occurrences in Scripture.

2 Chronicles 34:14 *And when they brought out the money that was brought into the house of the LORD, Hilkiah the priest found a book of the law of the LORD given by Moses.* **15** *And Hilkiah answered and said to Shaphan the scribe, I have found the book of the law in the house of the LORD. And Hilkiah delivered the book to Shaphan.*

Found. The priest "found" the book of the law of the LORD, the Pentateuch, Genesis through Deuteronomy. In order for it to have been found, it had to have first been lost. This godly king had been on the throne for eighteen years. He was twenty-six years old. And yet it seems that everything he was doing was simply because he had heard about it. All that the priests were doing was simply because they had heard about it. And yet hidden in the very house of God was a physical written copy of the word of God.

Of all the things that ought to never be lost, that one should be at the very top of the list for all of us! You see, while Josiah heard about the right things he should do and did them, Amon, his king and father before him, "heard about" the wrong things he should do and did them, believing them to be right!

The written Word of God must always be our absolute authority; DO make it so in your own life!

Personal Notes:

Devotion 80

The Word of God that was finally found in the house of God was brought to the king and read aloud before him. Look at what happened at that point.

2 Chronicles 34:19 *And it came to pass, when the king had heard the words of the law, that he rent his clothes.* **20** *And the king commanded Hilkiah, and Ahikam the son of Shaphan, and Abdon the son of Micah, and Shaphan the scribe, and Asaiah a servant of the king's, saying,* **21** *Go, enquire of the LORD for me, and for them that are left in Israel and in Judah, concerning the words of the book that is found: for great is the wrath of the LORD that is poured out upon us, because our fathers have not kept the word of the LORD, to do after all that is written in this book.*

Please remember that this was a very good and godly king, maybe the best one they ever had! And yet when he heard the words of the written Word of God, he immediately realized that everyone was in a lot of trouble. Those who came before him had sinned grievously, and because of that, everyone was under condemnation.

In that, this becomes a pretty good picture of our own case. No matter how "good" we are, we are all under condemnation because Adam, who came before us and violated God's law. And this is why we should be so grateful that in our case the wrath of the Lord was poured out on Christ, not on us!

Josiah tore his clothes. We don't have to do that, because Christ had His clothes, and even His body, torn for us. DO look to the cross today and realize that Adam's sin, and yours, has been fully dealt with in Christ!

Personal Notes:

_____

_____

_____

_____

_____

_____

_____

_____

_____

_____

_____

_____

_____

_____

_____

_____

_____

_____

_____

_____

_____

_____

_____

_____

_____

Devotion 81

King Josiah instructed Hilkiah, the high priest, and Shaphan, the scribe, to go inquire of the LORD concerning the book of the law that had been found and concerning the judgment that the king rightly feared was coming due to the millennia-long disobedience of the people. So they did as they were instructed and went seeking for someone who could give them a word directly from the LORD. Look, though, at who they sought out and how it went.

2 Chronicles 34:22 *And Hilkiah, and they that the king had appointed, went to Huldah the prophetess, the wife of Shallum the son of Tikvath, the son of Hasrah, keeper of the wardrobe; (now she dwelt in Jerusalem in the college:) and they spake to her to that effect.* **23** *And she answered them, Thus saith the LORD God of Israel...*

Huldah was a prophetess during the same time period in which notable prophets such as Jeremiah and Zephaniah were also engaged in their own prophetic ministry. Yet the king, high priest, and scribe sought out this woman instead of those men.

No, a prophet is not the same thing as a New Testament pastor, and yes, the qualifications of a pastor limit that office to men. But this is a clear indication that women in the Bible were held in high esteem and that they still should be today. I actually heard a man sing a version of "I Saw the Light" recently which he had "cleverly" re-written to say, "She'll keep her mouth shut, even when she's right, cause, praise the Lord, she saw the light!"

To be blunt, joking or not, that is so stupid that it would have to improve a thousand percent to even arrive at stupid.

DO realize that God gave women brains, very good ones, sometimes even better than all of the men around them and that they are just as capable of "getting in touch with God" as any man anywhere!

Personal Notes:

_____

_____

_____

_____

_____

_____

_____

_____

_____

_____

_____

_____

_____

_____

_____

_____

_____

_____

_____

_____

_____

_____

Devotion 82

Here was the message that Huldah the prophetess sent back to King Josiah.

2 Chronicles 34:24 *Thus saith the LORD, Behold, I will bring evil upon this place, and upon the inhabitants thereof, even all the curses that are written in the book which they have read before the king of Judah:* **25** *Because they have forsaken me, and have burned incense unto other gods, that they might provoke me to anger with all the works of their hands; therefore my wrath shall be poured out upon this place, and shall not be quenched.* **26** *And as for the king of Judah, who sent you to enquire of the LORD, so shall ye say unto him, Thus saith the LORD God of Israel concerning the words which thou hast heard;* **27** *Because thine heart was tender, and thou didst humble thyself before God, when thou heardest his words against this place, and against the inhabitants thereof, and humbledst thyself before me, and didst rend thy clothes, and weep before me; I have even heard thee also, saith the LORD.* **28** *Behold, I will gather thee to thy fathers, and thou shalt be gathered to thy grave in peace, neither shall thine eyes see all the evil that I will bring upon this place, and upon the inhabitants of the same. So they brought the king word again.*

There came a point at which God's wrath was not going to be turned away from the land even if a godly king ascended to the throne and did everything absolutely right. But there never came a point at which a person who was willing to humble himself before God was not going to receive the mercy of God individually! A land may fall due to wickedness, but God will never entirely withhold his mercy from humble people within the land who give themselves wholly to God.

DO strive to revive our land, but more importantly, DO be so humble before God that you receive mercy whether the land is ever revived or not!

Personal Notes:

_____

_____

_____

_____

_____

_____

_____

_____

_____

_____

_____

_____

_____

_____

_____

_____

_____

_____

_____

_____

Devotion 83

Godly King Josiah now knew two things for sure. One, the judgment of God was eventually coming on the land. Two, God was going to show him mercy because he humbled himself before God. Notice how he responded to those two facts.

2 Chronicles 34:30 *And the king went up into the house of the LORD, and all the men of Judah, and the inhabitants of Jerusalem, and the priests, and the Levites, and all the people, great and small: and he read in their ears all the words of the book of the covenant that was found in the house of the LORD. **31** And the king stood in his place, and made a covenant before the LORD, to walk after the LORD, and to keep his commandments, and his testimonies, and his statutes, with all his heart, and with all his soul, to perform the words of the covenant which are written in this book. **32** And he caused all that were present in Jerusalem and Benjamin to stand to it. And the inhabitants of Jerusalem did according to the covenant of God, the God of their fathers. **33** And Josiah took away all the abominations out of all the countries that pertained to the children of Israel, and made all that were present in Israel to serve, even to serve the LORD their God. And all his days they departed not from following the LORD, the God of their fathers.*

Josiah received an assurance of mercy for himself and for the land from the Lord during his days. And that mercy motivated him to greater godliness and to greater passion for God. And that is exactly the way it should always be. The fact that Christ died to pay for our sins and saves us when we repent and receive Him should always be a motivating factor for personal, practical holiness in our lives and a passion for God that everyone around us can see.

Are you saved? Then DO live like it!

Personal Notes:

_____

_____

_____

_____

_____

_____

_____

_____

_____

_____

_____

_____

_____

_____

_____

_____

_____

_____

_____

_____

_____

Devotion 84

Josiah was still not done. This most remarkable of kings, a man who never wavered from that which was right, was still pushing forward in his walk with God.

2 Chronicles 35:1 *Moreover Josiah kept a passover unto the LORD in Jerusalem: and they killed the passover on the fourteenth day of the first month.* **2** *And he set the priests in their charges, and encouraged them to the service of the house of the LORD,*

After all of the big things that Josiah did, we read of something here that could be considered a small thing… but in reality, is not small, not at all. Having scheduled and arranged a Passover Feast for all of the people, Josiah set the priests in their areas of responsibilities and then he "encouraged them" to the service of the house of the LORD. He did not just put them in place and tell them what to do; he encouraged them.

Did these ministers have a responsibility to do what they were being asked to do? Yes, absolutely. But the fact that someone has a responsibility to do something does not mean that we should not encourage them in the doing of it! Sometimes a bit of encouragement is all people need to keep going forward and keep trying and keep working and not quit. How many times do people pack it all in, leaving shocked followers to say, "I had no idea anything was even wrong!"

DO make sure that never happens to those you know who are serving the Lord; DO encourage them!

Personal Notes:

_____

_____

_____

_____

_____

_____

_____

_____

_____

_____

_____

_____

_____

_____

_____

_____

_____

_____

_____

_____

_____

_____

_____

_____

_____

_____

_____

_____

Devotion 85

Josiah was quite possibly the best king Judah ever had. But he was something more than that; he was necessary. By that I mean, not only was he the best king they ever had, but he was the best king they ever had during a time when the standard operating procedure all around was wickedness rather than righteousness. He stood right and did right when it mattered most. He led a revival when it was most needed. And he was the rarest of the rare in that he did right consistently and did not have some notable sin laid to his charge near the end of his life as so many before him.

And that is what makes his lapse of judgment in a practical matter such a tragedy.

2 Chronicles 35:20 *After all this, when Josiah had prepared the temple, Necho king of Egypt came up to fight against Carchemish by Euphrates: and Josiah went out against him.* **21** *But he sent ambassadors to him, saying, What have I to do with thee, thou king of Judah? I come not against thee this day, but against the house wherewith I have war: for God commanded me to make haste: forbear thee from meddling with God, who is with me, that he destroy thee not.* **22** *Nevertheless Josiah would not turn his face from him, but disguised himself, that he might fight with him, and hearkened not unto the words of Necho from the mouth of God, and came to fight in the valley of Megiddo.* **23** *And the archers shot at king Josiah; and the king said to his servants, Have me away; for I am sore wounded.* **24** *His servants* *therefore took him out of that chariot, and put him in the second chariot that he had; and they brought him to Jerusalem, and he died, and was buried in one of the sepulchres of his fathers. And all Judah and Jerusalem mourned for Josiah.*

This was not Josiah's battle. He had no business being there. He broke no commandment by doing so, and it was not a matter of sin, but this practical mistake on his part not only cost him but the entire nation greatly.

We always need to be careful not just to do right morally, but also to be reasonable practically. Sin can ruin a person, but so can stupidity.

DO be righteous, but DO also be smart in all of your decisions!

Personal Notes:

_____

_____

_____

_____

_____

_____

_____

_____

_____

_____

_____

_____

_____

_____

_____

_____

Devotion 86

We now come to the closing words concerning the life of the great and godly King Josiah.

2 Chronicles 35:25 *And Jeremiah lamented for Josiah: and all the singing men and the singing women spake of Josiah in their lamentations to this day, and made them an ordinance in Israel: and, behold, they are written in the lamentations.* **26** *Now the rest of the acts of Josiah, and his goodness, according to that which was written in the law of the LORD,* **27** *And his deeds, first and last, behold, they are written in the book of the kings of Israel and Judah.*

Josiah was a king; Jeremiah was a prophet. Josiah was a member of the political class; Jeremiah was a member of the clergy. And yet when that king died, the preacher wept and mourned over him. In fact, he wrote what would be classified as a funeral dirge, and the people sang it for years.

This is an excellent reminder that believers are not to be isolated from politics or from any other necessary aspect of community life. We are often told today that there is to be a wall of separation that keeps God and His people out of politics, yet that weird belief is found neither in Scripture nor in the Constitution. If God's people stay out of politics, who, pray tell, will be left there?

DO be political. Run for office, pray for those who are in office, get to know them, put godly pressure on them, and mourn for any good ones lost!

Personal Notes:

Devotion 87

The days of the southern kingdom were waning fast. Godly Josiah was dead due to his foolish interference in a battle that did not belong to him. The people of the land were going to put the new king on the throne, and things did not work out well at all for their decision.

2 Chronicles 36:1 *Then the people of the land took Jehoahaz the son of Josiah, and made him king in his father's stead in Jerusalem. 2 Jehoahaz was twenty and three years old when he began to reign, and he reigned three months in Jerusalem. 3 And the king of Egypt put him down at Jerusalem, and condemned the land in an hundred talents of silver and a talent of gold. 4 And the king of Egypt made Eliakim his brother king over Judah and Jerusalem, and turned his name to Jehoiakim. And Necho took Jehoahaz his brother, and carried him to Egypt.*

Here is the progression. One, a godly king makes a foolish decision and dies way too young. Two, the king who comes in behind him quickly sweeps away the revival of his father and brings idolatry back to the land. Three, the king of a foreign nation invades the land, dethrones the king and takes him captive, and puts his own choice on the throne.

All of this took just three months.

In three months, they went from making their own decisions and having the blessings of God on their lives to being completely dominated and enslaved. People who play around with sin fail to realize how quickly it can cost them everything!

DO have enough sense to live for God every day of your life, unless you want the theme of your life to be "well, that went wrong in a hurry!"

Personal Notes:

_____

_____

_____

_____

_____

_____

_____

_____

_____

_____

_____

_____

_____

_____

_____

_____

_____

_____

_____

_____

_____

_____

_____

_____

_____

Devotion 88

We now arrive at some of the most heartbreaking words in Scripture in light of the glorious promises of God to Israel.

2 Chronicles 36:5 *Jehoiakim was twenty and five years old when he began to reign, and he reigned eleven years in Jerusalem: and he did that which was evil in the sight of the LORD his God.* **6** *Against him came up Nebuchadnezzar king of Babylon, and bound him in fetters, to carry him to Babylon.*

One small detail to clear up is that though Nebuchadnezzar came against Jehoiakim and bound him in fetters with the purpose of bringing him to Babylon, he did not actually follow through with that purpose. Instead, he allowed Jehoiakim to remain as a tribute king. Just a few years later he was killed by the Assyrians. But the main thing to notice from this passage is that Nebuchadnezzar was now marching against Jerusalem and taking people into bondage. This would ultimately lead to the horrible seventy-year captivity of Israel in Babylon. The nation that God had redeemed from Egypt by His strong right hand, the nation that He had given the land of Canaan as an inheritance, the nation that could literally have stood forever if they had simply obeyed, was now destroyed.

Oh, how much people lose by their rebellion against God!

Do you want to be blessed and helped by the God of heaven? Then DO obey Him! He is not a genie in a bottle to grant wishes to whoever says the magic

words; He is the sovereign and holy God who
instituted the law of sowing and reaping!

Personal Notes:

_____

_____

_____

_____

_____

_____

_____

_____

_____

_____

_____

_____

_____

_____

_____

_____

_____

_____

_____

_____

_____

_____

_____

_____

_____

_____

Devotion 89

The final days of Judah's monarchy were an absolute train wreck. Jehoiakim was now gone, and here is the next disaster of a king that they dealt with.

2 Chronicles 36:8 *Now the rest of the acts of Jehoiakim, and his abominations which he did, and that which was found in him, behold, they are written in the book of the kings of Israel and Judah: and Jehoiachin his son reigned in his stead.* **9** *Jehoiachin was eight years old when he began to reign, and he reigned three months and ten days in Jerusalem: and he did that which was evil in the sight of the LORD.* **10** *And when the year was expired, king Nebuchadnezzar sent, and brought him to Babylon, with the goodly vessels of the house of the LORD, and made Zedekiah his brother king over Judah and Jerusalem.*

Please allow me to summarize these verses: Judah ended up with an eight-year-old brat on the throne as their king. If you think being ruled by a horrible adult is bad, imagine being ruled by a horrible child! And in short order, brat-boy was taken into captivity in Babylon. But even worse, he somehow got under Nebuchadnezzar's skin so badly that Nebuchadnezzar also took the precious vessels out of the house of the Lord into Babylon along with brat-boy.

None of us are earthly king, but most all of us have a family of some type. And those unfortunate families who find themselves "ruled by brats" are some of the most pitiable people on earth! Parents, if

God had intended your children to rule the home, they would have given birth to you, not vice versa. So DO be in charge in your home, and DO demand that your children have both proper actions and proper attitudes!

Personal Notes:

_____

_____

_____

_____

_____

_____

_____

_____

_____

_____

_____

_____

_____

_____

_____

_____

_____

_____

_____

_____

_____

_____

_____

_____

_____

_____

Devotion 90

Once brat-boy was deposed, Nebuchadnezzar put his older brother, Zedekiah (who before this was called Mattaniah), on the throne in Jerusalem as the new tribute king. The expectation was the same: mind your manners and do not cause any trouble. Interestingly, that was pretty much God's expectation for him as well. But, and I know this is shocking, Zedekiah was wicked and stubborn and refused to do right.

2 Chronicles 36:11 *Zedekiah was one and twenty years old when he began to reign, and reigned eleven years in Jerusalem.* **12** *And he did that which was evil in the sight of the LORD his God, and humbled not himself before Jeremiah the prophet speaking from the mouth of the LORD.* **13** *And he also rebelled against king Nebuchadnezzar, who had made him swear by God: but he stiffened his neck, and hardened his heart from turning unto the LORD God of Israel.* **14** *Moreover all the chief of the priests, and the people, transgressed very much after all the abominations of the heathen; and polluted the house of the LORD which he had hallowed in Jerusalem.* **15** *And the LORD God of their fathers sent to them by his messengers, rising up betimes, and sending; because he had compassion on his people, and on his dwelling place:* **16** *But they mocked the messengers of God, and despised his words, and misused his prophets, until the wrath of the LORD arose against his people, till there was no remedy.*

Zedekiah is specifically said to have rebelled against God, against Jeremiah the man of God, and against several unnamed prophets of God. Simply put, no one could tell him anything. He was like those frustrating people today who say, "Only God can judge me!" without even actually believing that God can judge them. No preacher, no parent, no one can correct them.

And what was the end result? Verse sixteen says, *"The wrath of the LORD arose against his people, till there was no remedy."*

No remedy... those are frightening words! DO be willing to listen and take correction; "remedy" has an expiration date, and once that date comes, all that is left is judgment!

Personal Notes:

_____

_____

_____

_____

_____

_____

_____

_____

_____

_____

_____

_____

_____

_____

_____

Devotion 91

Having wearied God to the point of no remedy, King Zedekiah and Judah now faced the third and final invasion of Jerusalem by Nebuchadnezzar, King of Babylon. The results were going to be horrific.

2 Chronicles 36:17 *Therefore he brought upon them the king of the Chaldees, who slew their young men with the sword in the house of their sanctuary, and had no compassion upon young man or maiden, old man, or him that stooped for age: he gave them all into his hand.* **18** *And all the vessels of the house of God, great and small, and the treasures of the house of the LORD, and the treasures of the king, and of his princes; all these he brought to Babylon.* **19** *And they burnt the house of God, and brake down the wall of Jerusalem, and burnt all the palaces thereof with fire, and destroyed all the goodly vessels thereof.* **20** *And them that had escaped from the sword carried he away to Babylon; where they were servants to him and his sons until the reign of the kingdom of Persia:* **21** *To fulfil the word of the LORD by the mouth of Jeremiah, until the land had enjoyed her sabbaths: for as long as she lay desolate she kept sabbath, to fulfil threescore and ten years.*

The most glorious structure ever built on earth was the magnificent Temple of Solomon. This place, around which the heart of the entire nation revolved, was burned to the ground. The walls of Jerusalem were completely broken down. All of the palaces were burned down. All of the wealth was taken away.

Many of the people of the land were taken into captivity. For seventy years, Judah would pay the price for their rebellion against God.

God began their monarchy, and God ended it. We would do well to remember that others will either be blessed by our obedience or hurt by our disobedience. The kings called the shots, but the people paid the price. DO live in such a way that people around you can be free and blessed rather than ruined!

Personal Notes:

_____

_____

_____

_____

_____

_____

_____

_____

_____

_____

_____

_____

_____

_____

_____

_____

_____

_____

_____

_____

Devotion 92

As we arrive in the very last two verses of the book of 2 Chronicles, you should very quickly be able to tell that a large gap of time has simply been skipped over in order to arrive at a more blessed time:

2 Chronicles 36:22 *Now in the first year of Cyrus king of Persia, that the word of the LORD spoken by the mouth of Jeremiah might be accomplished, the LORD stirred up the spirit of Cyrus king of Persia, that he made a proclamation throughout all his kingdom, and put it also in writing, saying,* **23** *Thus saith Cyrus king of Persia, All the kingdoms of the earth hath the LORD God of heaven given me; and he hath charged me to build him an house in Jerusalem, which is in Judah. Who is there among you of all his people? The LORD his God be with him, and let him go up.*

The entire seventy-year captivity fits between verses twenty-one and twenty-two. The last thing we saw in the text was Nebuchadnezzar leveling Jerusalem and burning the Temple to the ground. Now we see a new king and a new kingdom over all the earth, Cyrus and Persia. Just as God prophesied, the captivity was exactly seventy years, and a king named Cyrus would release the people and commission the building of a new Temple. Politically speaking, this was a bad move for Cyrus; there was no logical reason for him to do it. He did it, in his words, specifically because the LORD God of heaven told him to do so.

Do you often feel like politics and politicians are beyond anyone's reach and influence? Do you feel frustrated that they never seem to have to answer to anyone? The truth of the matter is, no one is beyond God's reach and influence, and everyone will answer to Him. If He chooses to do so, he can use even a wicked king for a godly purpose. So what should this tell you about your prayer life?

DO pray and believe that God has power even over the affairs of men; while He owes us nothing, when He chooses to do so, He can move the entire world with just a word!

Personal Notes:

_____

_____

_____

_____

_____

_____

_____

_____

_____

_____

_____

_____

_____

_____

_____

_____

_____

_____

Books in the Night Heroes Series

Cry From the Coal Mine (Vol. 1)
Free Fall (Vol. 2)
Broken Brotherhood (Vol. 3)
The Blade of Black Crow (Vol. 4)
Ghost Ship (Vol. 5)
When Serpents Rise (Vol. 6)
Moth Man (Vol. 7)
Runaway (Vol. 8)
Terror by Day (Vol. 9)
Winter Wolf (Vol. 10)

More Books by Dr. Bo Wagner

Beyond the Colored Coat
Don't Muzzle the Ox
From Footers to Finish Nails
I'm Saved! Now What???
Learning Not to Fear the Old Testament
Marriage Makers/Marriage Breakers

Daniel: Breathtaking
Esther: Five Feast and the Fingerprints of God
James: The Pen and the Plumb Line
Jonah: A Study in Greatness
Nehemiah: A Labor of Love
Proverbs: Bright Lights from Dark Sayings Vol 1
Proverbs: Bright Lights from Dark Sayings Vol 2
Romans: Salvation From A-Z
Ruth: Diamonds in the Darkness
The Revelation: Ready or Not

Devotionals

DO Drops Volume 1
DO Drops Volume 2
DO Drops Volume 3
DO Drops Volume 4
DO Drops Volume 5
DO Drops Volume 6
DO Drops Volume 7
DO Drops Volume 8

Sci-Fi

Zak Blue and the Great Space Chase Series:
Falcon Wing (Vol. 1)
Enter the Maelstrom (Vol. 2)

www.ingramcontent.com/pod-product-compliance
Lightning Source LLC
Chambersburg PA
CBHW060155070426
42447CB00033B/1468